JESUS *the* TEACHER

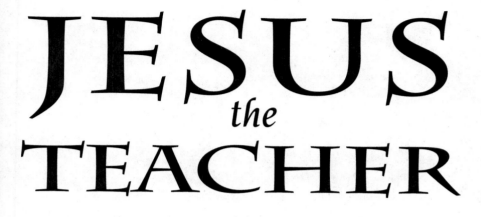

JESUS *the* TEACHER

Examining His Expertise in Education

Herman Horne

Revised and Updated by Angus M. Gunn

kregel
PUBLICATIONS

Grand Rapids, MI 49501

Library of Congress Cataloging-in-Publication Data
Horne, Herman Harrell, 1874–1946.
 Jesus the teacher: examining his expertise in education / by Herman Harrell Horne.
  p.   cm.
 Revised edition of: Jesus, the master teacher. 1920.
 Includes bibliographical references.
 1. Jesus Christ teaching methods. I. Gunn, Angus M. (Angus Macleod), 1920– . II. Horne, Herman Harrell, 1874–1946. Jesus, the master teacher. III. Title.
BT590.T5H7   1998   232.9'04—dc21   98-42201
                                                CIP

ISBN 978-0-8254-2859-3

Printed in the United States of America

3 4 5 6 7 / 13 12 11 10 09

CONTENTS

LIST OF FIGURES

INTRODUCTION

Conditions in North American classrooms changed dramatically in the last quarter of the twentieth century. Instead of the uniform curricula of earlier times there was a range of programs. The melting-pot philosophy of community, so dear to John Dewey and others, gave way to a mosaic of multiethnic societies. These social changes, coupled with the impact of television and computers, revolutionized both the content and the process of learning. Traditional values and practices were frequently rejected.

There was no easy consensus on alternatives, on what to transmit to a succeeding generation. Which values and what accomplishments from the past ought to be treasured? What may be rejected? How can excellence be achieved? Where are the guidelines for teachers? What can we learn from educational research?

Cracks in traditional education began to appear in the 1960s, when research reports from Britain and the United States showed that parents can exercise critical influences on performance in school. In the 1970s came further shocks, the findings on exemplary schools. The positive influence on student achievement of an orderly, harmonious school environment was discovered. Recognition of the necessity of value consensus soon followed.

The same research that revealed the critical role of parents, society, and value consensus also identified the new kinds of pedagogy needed. Student investigation replaced teacher-centered rote learning. Open-ended inquiry took over from Socratic-style questioning. Above all, good interpersonal relationships became essential. New findings on brain research emphasized the importance of these relationships. Mutual trust between student and teacher, coupled with a caring attitude on the part of the teacher, guarantee high achievement and are a necessity when one is dealing with culturally disadvantaged students.

Where can we find models of teaching that match these demands? Inexorably, the quest takes us back to antiquity, to first-century Palestine, where Jesus demonstrated styles of teaching, albeit only partially developed, that were as well suited to the multiethnic world of his time as they are to ours. It would be hard to find an equally good model since that time. The values he cherished and gave to posterity in the form of the Judeo-Christian ethic have been a guiding light in the development of western civilization. They remain the indispensable foundation for good education today.

Jesus lived in a world of ethical confusion. Greek and other cultures had changed the ancient Jewish traditions. Nevertheless, Jesus taught successfully in this environment by preserving what was best from the past and extending it in new ways. Most of his work was not understood by his contemporaries because he was so far ahead of his time. With hindsight we can see that his pedagogy meets the highest demands of modern educational practice.

Herman Harrell Horne was the first educator in modern times to recognize both the value and relevance of Jesus as a teacher and the features of his pedagogy that were superior to those prevailing in the public schools of the United States. This book is an eloquent testimony to Horne's understanding of the former, that is, to Jesus as a teacher, but we need to look further afield, into Horne's life and his other publications, if we are going to grasp the extent of his influence over the educational world of the 1920s and 1930s.

Horne was born in Clayton, North Carolina, on November 22, 1874, a third-generation son of a Scottish immigrant. Following school and university studies in his home state (he earned two degrees from the University of North Carolina by the age of twenty-two), he went on to Harvard to complete his Ph.D. two years later, in 1899. His thesis, "History and Philosophy of the Problem of Sin," set the stage for an illustrious career in teaching and writing on many aspects of education and Christian faith. By 1906 his first two major books, *The Philosophy of Education* and *Psychological Principles of Education*, were published by the Macmillan Company of New York. The academic year 1906–1907 was spent in postgraduate study at the University of Berlin.

In 1909 Horne was appointed professor of philosophy of education at the University of New York (NYU), an appointment later extended to include professor of the history of education. He remained at NYU until his retirement as professor emeritus in 1942. During his tenure at NYU almost all of his books were written and his influence on education peaked. See the bibliography at the end of this book for a list of his major works. Foremost among these books, and the one in which he was most interested, is the original version of this one, first published in 1920 under the title *Jesus, the Master Teacher.* It is a fitting tribute to its quality that the essential content of that first edition remains unchanged.

Horne's dedication to public education was no less strong than his devotion to the pedagogy of the Gospels. He spoke all across the United States on issues that affected the schools. *The Democratic Philosophy of Education*, a best-seller in its time and one that was translated into several languages, is the outstanding example of his contributions to educational thought. This book is a critique of another no less famous book, *Democracy and Education*, written by the nation's leading educator, John Dewey. Cambridge University's department of philosophy, along with numerous scholarly journals in different parts of Europe and the United States, wrote approvingly of Horne's book.

In his comments on the central theme of Dewey's book, Horne says, "Dewey's definition of democracy fails to take adequate account of the obstacles in the way of achieving his defined democracy. Others have recognized them: indifference of the voter, unreliability of the press, the power of propaganda, the inability of the school alone to solve all problems, and the self-seeking politicians." The point about school alone not being able to solve problems is a familiar fact now. In Horne's time it was nothing short of prophetic. This very weakness in Dewey's philosophy led ultimately to the collapse of his educational methodology.

Horne was accorded many honors in the course of his time at NYU. He was a much sought-after speaker in colleges and summer institutes. He was awarded four honorary LL.D. degrees from four different universities. He was the first university professor to broadcast a classroom lecture by radio. That was in 1923 under the auspices of the New York University School of the Air. His numerous professional associations included being a fellow of the American Association for the Advancement of Science and holding memberships in the Society for the Advancement of Education, American Philosophical Association, American Academy of Political and Social Sciences, and the Society of College Teachers of Education.

In early years Horne was a Baptist, but his later religious affiliation was with the Presbyterian church. Politically he was a Democrat. He enjoyed all kinds of outdoor activities—swimming, fishing, tennis, and golf. He was twice married, first to Alice Elizabeth Herbert. She died in 1934, leaving four children. His second wife was Mary Dowell Williamson. Horne died in Leonia, New Jersey, on August 16, 1946.

In the first edition of this book Horne made it clear that it was not a book to be read so much as a guide to be followed in study classes. It was especially designed for discussion groups. He consistently stressed that his viewpoint was not the content of Jesus' teaching but rather the form in which the content is cast. This was how he described his teaching method: "The mode of presentation will, so far as possible, make the reader a sharer in the process of discovering the methods of Jesus as a teacher. This result will be accomplished by first raising questions, then giving the reader a chance to answer them tentatively for himself or herself, and finally presenting additional material to reach a more considered conclusion." This is the method that is found in this new edition.

Angus M. Gunn

1

TEACHING

We are going to study "how Jesus taught." This implies that he was acquainted with the teaching situation, even that he was a part of it and faced its problems, and that he was confronted with the same kinds of difficulties in teaching as we are, if not the identical ones. That he clearly sensed teaching as a problem appears in the parable of the sower, which exemplifies four kinds of students.

Now what are the elements essentially involved in the teaching situation? It is an easy question, and if you would be an independent student, pause here and first make the analysis for yourself, then read on. The teaching situation involves (1) a teacher, (2) students, (3) environment, (4) curriculum, (5) aims, and (6) method.

Can you think of any additional essential thing? Can these six be further reduced?

Were the teaching situations in which Jesus found himself ever complex enough to contain these six elements? Take, for example, the scene of Jesus and Nicodemus, under the olive trees at night on the mount near Jerusalem. Jesus was the teacher, addressed by the student, Nicodemus, as follows: "Rabbi, we know you are a teacher who has come from God" (John 3:2). The environment is that night scene, protecting a distinguished but timid and fearful student. The curriculum is "the birth from above." The aim of the teacher was probably to effect a great change in the life of his student. Was this aim accomplished? See John 7:50 and 19:39. The method used was conversation, including questions and answers and a remarkable concrete illustration of the working of the Spirit (John 3:8).

Analyze another one of the teaching situations in the life of Jesus, that with the woman of Samaria (John 4:1-42).

In fact, would it not help us to make a list as complete as possible of all the leading teaching situations in the life of Jesus?

Would it be proper to regard the miracles he wrought as teaching situations? For the answer, see Mark 2:10 and study Luke 5:1-11.

If the miracle situation is not to be regarded as primarily a teaching situation, may it be so regarded in a secondary sense? Why? This question implies that the miracles may have taught the people lessons without being done for that purpose. We get the unavoidable impression that Jesus was repeatedly involved in teaching. The following studies will concentrate on the ways he taught.

2

A CASE STUDY

Later we shall take one principle of teaching and seek illustrations of it in the work of Jesus. Now we propose at the outset to take one part of his work, a unity in itself, and find in it some of the principles and methods of teaching he utilized. It will give us an overview of the field.

As a general rule, Jesus did not try to give us object lessons in teaching (he did on one occasion wash the disciples' feet to give them an object lesson in humility) but rather to provide masterly lessons for his disciples that would serve as models for their own study.

What would be a good illustration to take? Select your own and find in it all the principles of teaching you can.

Let us choose John 4:1–42.

Topic: How Jesus taught the woman of Samaria.

1. Here we have a complete teaching situation, with teacher, student, environment, curriculum, aim, and method. Jesus is the teacher, the woman of Samaria is the student, Jacob's well is a part of the environment, the water of life is a part of the curriculum, and the transforming of a life the aim. Now, what are the methods?
2. The teacher utilized a teachable moment, though he was weary with his journey, and it was the noon hour, and she was a Samaritan and a woman. There were several reasons why he might have let this occasion slip, but he did not. "A Samaritan woman came to draw water."
3. She had evidently come to draw water. Jesus said to her, "Will you give me a drink?" He was thirsty; it was a natural request.

13

4. He had her attention and interest from the start. He had done an unexpected and unusual thing. He utilized surprise power. Though a Jew, he had spoken to a Samaritan. This attention and interest are sustained throughout, even increasing in concentration and intensity as slumbering impulses are awakened.
5. He used the conversational method. Seven times he addressed her and six times she replied, the arrival of the disciples interrupting the conversation.
6. He was dealing with an individual, though the way was opened to deal with the crowds of her city for two days.
7. He exemplified the principle of modeling, for a brief time, by intimate conversation with a woman, causing his disciples to marvel.
8. He asked her no question, but he answered three of her explicit questions, as well as her deepest longing. He built upon her answers and made the most of them: "You are right."
9. There are problems at the basis of this teaching. First, there are the personal needs in the woman's life. Who was more conscious of this at first, the woman or Jesus? It was his object to awaken her conscience. Then there is the theological problem, felt and stated by the woman: Where shall God be worshiped? She seems to have introduced this problem as a distraction from the personal issue, but the answer of Jesus, "in spirit and in truth," reopened the personal problem.

Are there still other problems here? Which ones?

10. His reply concerning the nature of worship and God is perhaps long enough to be regarded as the nucleus of a private conversation with a single listener. How did John learn about this conversation, do you suppose?
11. There is the use of a familiar referent in passing from water to "living water," yet it is clear that even so the woman did not understand (see v. 15). There is a good referent also in Jesus declaring himself to be the Messiah to one who said she knew that Messiah is coming (vv. 25-26), and this time she evidently understood.
12. His use of the concrete appears in "to drink," "this water," "your husband," "five husbands," "this mountain," "Jerusalem," "I am he." The concrete water of Jacob's well was used to illustrate the abstract water of life.

13. His use of contrast appears in the difference between "this water," after drinking of which one thirsts again, and his living water, after drinking of which one shall never thirst (vv. 13–14). Also there is contrast between the ignorant worship of the Samaritans and the intelligent worship of the Jews (v. 22).

14. His use of motivation appears in the awakening first of interest and then of conscience and finally of service. The conversation concerning water awakened interest, that concerning the husband awakened conscience, that concerning true worship awakened service. She carried back in haste to the city, not the waterpot she had brought, but the living water.

15. Jesus secured action from this woman, first in words and then in deeds. He pierced her conscience by a command to act: "Go, call your husband and come back." A command that could not be executed is the profound way in which the teacher threw this woman back upon herself. Unintelligently she said: "Sir, give me this water"; intelligently she said: "Sir, I can see that you are a prophet." From superficial questions of curiosity her self-expression passes to serious concern in personal and religious matters and finally to the ministry in Sychar.

16. Some striking characteristics of Jesus as a teacher appear in this incident, such as his disregard of current conventionality in talking with a Samaritan and a woman; the absence of false modesty; intimate knowledge of his student (how did Jesus know the woman had had five husbands?); profound knowledge of his subject—the nature of God as spiritual; the demonstrated ability to teach; prophecy, "a time is coming"; and self-assertion: "I who speak to you am he."

What impressions do you get from this evidence of teaching method in a single incident?

Do you feel that any one of these sixteen points is not really to be found in the case?

Would you add still other evidence of teaching method?

Take another one of the several longer conversations of Jesus, and see what principles of teaching you can find there also.

Is it better to study one teaching incident in the light of the principles or to study one principle at a time in the light of many illustrative incidents? In the former case there is repetition of principles as we pass from incident to incident; in the latter case there is repetition of references to the same incidents as we pass from principle to principle. Which method does this book mainly follow?

Take the conversation with Nicodemus and work out results similar to the ones above.

3

EDUCATIONAL AIMS

A real teacher must have both strategy and tactics, that is, he must have both objectives and means for attaining them. Without strategy, tactics have no goal; without tactics, strategy has no means of attainment.

What were the objectives of the great teacher?

First, make a list of these for yourself, and then compare it with the one given below.

1. To do his Father's will and work. "My food is to do the will of him who sent me and to finish his work" (John 4:34).
2. To be accepted as the Messiah. "I who speak to you am he." "Who do you say I am?"
3. To win learners and to train them as witnesses of his. So he called many, and chose a few to be apostles, and sent them out two by two, and said to them: "You are my witnesses."
4. To substitute vital for formal religion. This covers a great deal, including the prayer of the publican, the benevolence of the poor widow, fasting in secret, the elimination of the motives of murder and lust and hatred, perhaps even the destruction of the sacrificial system in the cleansing of the temple. "I desire mercy, not sacrifice." "Pray to your Father, who is unseen."
5. To fulfill the law in the new universal kingdom of social righteousness. "Do not think that I have come to abolish the Law or the Prophets; I have not come to abolish them but to fulfill them." Most of the parables were designed to make plain to discerning minds the nature of the kingdom.

6. To show by example and to teach by precept the way of life. "I have come that they may have life, and have it to the full." Through seeking and saving the lost, he would prevent the ultimate miscarriage of life. He came to bear witness to the truth that by losing life we gain it. He gave his life as a ransom for many.
7. To quicken the faith and hope of men. He added to John the Baptist's gospel of repentance the injunction: "Believe the gospel," that is, accept as true the good news of God's love and act accordingly. His concern was that at his coming again he should find faith on the earth.
8. To break the bonds of racial prejudice. He talked with a Samaritan woman at high noon. He made a Samaritan the model neighbor in one of his stories. He healed the daughter of a Syrophoenician woman and the servant of a Roman centurion. He received Greeks and spoke to them of life through death. He talked of his "other sheep," of the leavening of "the whole," of the salt of "the earth," of the light of the "world."
9. To destroy the works of darkness. Thus by the finger of God he cast out demons, healed diseases, and relieved affliction of every kind, and gave his disciples power and authority over demons.

How would you extend this list?

Note we have here read his aims in terms of his accomplishments. Is this justifiable? If so, why? If not, what were his aims as distinct from his accomplishments?

Which of these aims are practicable for his followers today?

In his aims as a teacher, did Jesus place primary emphasis on the acting or the thinking of his students?

The statement of aims given above is drawn from his own teachings. Suppose we approach the matter from another angle. Make a list of the aims of education as a present-day thinker might formulate them. Then consider the extent to which these aims appear in the deeds and words of Jesus. Such a mode of procedure would apply a modern standard to work done nearly twenty centuries ago.

The aims of education:

1. To train in physical fitness
2. To develop good character
3. To express affective understanding

4. To equip young people to think
5. To make a good citizen
6. To learn practical skills
7. To relate life to its source and goal

It is true that such a statement as this is synthetic. It probably would not be found in its entirety in the usual books today on educational theory. Points three and seven are very commonly omitted. But it is a fair composite picture of what educators hold concerning the aims of education.

Now ask yourself the question: To what extent do these aims appear in the work of Jesus as teacher?

1. He healed the bodies of men and made them whole.
2. He lived and taught the highest standards of moral character.
3. He pointed out the beauties of nature.
4. He taught ethical and spiritual truths and trained the minds of his disciples.
5. He was a good citizen and taught obedience to civil authority.
6. He was a carpenter and taught the economic virtues.
7. He was the Son, and he taught the spiritual content of life.

We note then that Jesus practiced what many educators say, that complete education is sevenfold: physical, moral, esthetic, intellectual, social, vocational, and spiritual. In both practice and theory the master teacher long ago set up standards that are also those of good pedagogy today.

What comments do you wish to make on this?

The great objective of Jesus was to bring men to attain, or at least to approximate, his own state of mind. This objective led him to become a teacher, and the difficulty of his task determined his methods, for example, training a few, being reticent, and healing men and women. People would be brought to recognize him for what he was without his open avowal of divine sonship, a claim that some would regard as blasphemous and others as insane talk. He faced all this at the time of the temptation.

Would you say that one of the aims of Jesus was to establish religion as an ecclesiastical institution on the earth?

Did Jesus intend to reform Judaism or to found Christianity?

Review his aims and ask in which he succeeded best.

To what extent should his aims be ours?

4

OPENERS

When one mind approaches another for any reason, the first thing to do is to catch attention. Openers in human contacts are often secured by a word, a gesture, or a touch. The need of winning attention and of keeping it is felt not only by the teacher before his class but also by the preacher before his congregation, the lecturer before his audience, the lawyer before his jury, the salesman before his purchaser, and even the writer and the advertiser, though only the printed page is before their readers. Anyone who seeks to influence another must first have that person's attention.

Did Jesus have the attention of his listeners and also those who did not hear him but only heard of him? Who since his day has so successfully secured the attention of humanity? Stop for a few minutes to think about your answers to these questions.

Why was this? How did Jesus so capture the attention of his generation and, we may add, of all generations? For he is a teacher of the world.

What kind of attention did Jesus receive? What kind did his disciples (learners) give him? What kind did the Pharisees give him? Some who came to scoff remained to pray. With what kind of attention did they begin and end?

These questions you will probably find no trouble in answering. Jesus received plenty of attention. His own disciples attended willingly. His critics, hearing him, not because they wanted to obey but to entrap him in his talk, gave him attention. Pilate's wife, but glimpsing him perhaps, gave attention. Pilate, with no interest in the proceedings instituted by the ecclesiastical Jews but rather a distaste for the whole business, gave attention. Those sent to take him, returning without him but with the reason that "no man ever spoke like this man," ended by giving him attention, as did those Jews who believed in him secretly, not openly, for fear of the ridicule of their fellows. The multitude gave him attention, "hearing him gladly." The people of Nazareth, with "eyes fastened upon him" in the synagogue, began by giving him attention, though it changed as they drew back from the greatness of his claim.

What kind of attention was that of Nicodemus? of the woman of Samaria? of the men of Sychar? of the Gadarenes? of Herod? of Mary, the sister of Lazarus?

Now, how did Jesus secure attention? It was no great problem to him. "He could not be hid." He secured attention because first, there were many things about him to interest people; second, he knew what to do to get attention.

What are some of the things he did to get attention?

He called for it. Hear, listen, behold, give ear, he would say.

He announced his coming to any city by messengers sent in advance: the disciples who went into every city where he himself was about to come.

He utilized posture, not that he ever posed. "He sat down [the position of a Jewish teacher]. His disciples came to him, and he began to teach them." He would sit in a boat on a lake and teach people who were on the shore.

He spoke in concrete, pictorial, imaginative language, which easily catches and holds the attention, as a moving picture does today. The phrase "fishers of men" may rivet the attention like a fixed idea.

He used the familiar to explain the unfamiliar. Thus he said men do not put new wine into old bottles to explain why he and his disciples, contrary to the custom of John and his disciples, did not fast. There is a saying, "The new in the old is what excites interest." Did Jesus exemplify this canon? Can you illustrate your answer?

In teaching he did not overemphasize a point but passed quickly from one phase to another of his general topic. Thus, the different brief beatitudes. So, too, parables were spoken successively, one story after another, as the lost sheep, the lost coin, the lost son. Here is unity in variety. It has been said that the subject must change to win attention. Does Jesus exemplify this maxim? Can you give other illustrations?

Jesus also won attention because his teaching was so different from that of the scribes. "He taught as one who had authority, and not as their teachers of the law." Why will men listen more readily to one who speaks with authority (the prophet) than to one who speaks for the authorities (the priest)?

We may also say that Jesus received attention because he paid attention. He saw and was interested in what people were doing and saying and in their needs, and in helpful sympathy he empathized with them. His works prepared the way for his words.

And people gave him attention because he was a peripatetic teacher. He taught as he journeyed from place to place. "We must go into the next towns," he would say. Protagoras, the Greek Sophist, and Aristotle, the Greek philosopher, walked with their students within enclosures. Jesus walked with his students in the open, carrying good news to all.

But mainly Jesus won attention because of that complex thing that we call personal magnetism. The sum of his qualities made him unique, matchless, winsome. People would say he had not been taught in the rabbinical school in Jerusalem, that he came from Galilee, not Judea, that he was a Nazarene, that he was more than a match for the scribes, that he was followed by crowds, and that he was always doing and saying wonderful things. In short, the personality of Jesus attracted the attention of men.

Not that Jesus was, and did, and said all these things consciously and intentionally to get the attention of men. Winning and keeping attention was probably not a problem to him at all. He simply and naturally did those attention-winning things that poorer teachers must do with set purpose. Thus we must consciously imitate him as our model.

Can you now think of other ways in which Jesus won attention?

The point that it was mainly through personal magnetism that Jesus secured attention, just as any good painting of him today arrests our attention, leads us naturally to ask: What in Jesus interested people?

Suppose you had the privilege of presenting one request to Jesus face to face, what would it be? Or, of asking him one question, what would it be? What question would you like to ask Socrates? Think about the answers to these questions. They will disclose to you the deeper sources of your own interest in Jesus.

The personality of Jesus was so striking that men, with their expectation of a Messiah to come, would say of him, "Can this be Messiah?" "When Messiah comes, will he do more wonderful things than this man?" But others would say, "You are a Samaritan and demon-possessed." So the people of Palestine were interested in fitting Jesus into their own views of life. It was the habit of Jesus to let people freely see in him the Messiah for whom they looked rather than publicly to proclaim it, though he did the latter also, by implication, in the synagogue at Nazareth. So his messiahship interested people.

Along with this went his claim to be able to forgive sins on earth. He even taught his disciples to bind and to loosen on earth. This is an arresting claim that would naturally concern people in a practical way and their rulers in a theological way.

Then, too, the exalted content of his message interested the people. Accustomed to legalism as they were, here was a teaching of love that fulfilled all law, of mercy that was more than animal sacrifice, of a loving Father who saved and did not condemn the world.

Also they were attracted by the wonderful signs he wrought, which he did in loving and helpful sympathy, not just to convince people of his messiahship. In fact, the crowds would so follow him because of his works and also to get the loaves and fishes and be filled, that it was his custom to forbid the miraculously healed people to tell others. This, however, only caused some to publish it yet the more. So the fame of him would spread as a wonder worker, but he knew the nature of people and would not trust himself to those who had no better basis for belief. So Herod in his palace heard of him and desired in kingly curiosity to see some magical work by him. This, together with Herod's evil treatment of John, were so distasteful to Jesus that he said nothing. It was one of the times when even the silence of Jesus spoke with eloquence. But unquestionably the people continued to treat Jesus as a wonder worker, though he did not care for such regard.

A thing that always characterized Jesus and that never failed to interest high and low alike was his social freedom. He mingled with publicans and sinners, ate with them, received them, was known as their "friend," and so scandalized the leaders. But he was equally at home in the house of Simon the Pharisee at Bethany, and while he was there he permitted gracious social attention from a forgiven street woman. Besides, though keeping both letter and spirit of the Law of Moses, he paid no attention to the traditions of the elders about ceremonial cleansings of pots and vessels, eating with washed hands, not husking grain on the Sabbath day, and so on. He was above the established good usage, both religious and social, of his day. This social freedom interested everyone.

What additional things about Jesus would naturally interest people? The fact that to some he extended a definite call to be with him? His moral earnestness? How would you explain the fact that the young fishermen accepted his invitation at once? Why did the young ruler decline? What do you suppose would have happened if Jesus and Saul of Tarsus had met face to face in the flesh? What do you think would happen now if Jesus should visit in the flesh one of our towns or cities as he visited Capernaum or Jerusalem? Would he have our attention? In what would we be interested? How much has human nature changed in twenty centuries?

We have seen in a measure how the problem of attention and interest was solved in the teaching of Jesus. Make a list of the points he exemplified that we may imitate more or less in our work as teachers. Do you find that it brings Jesus too near or makes him too real in flesh and blood to study him in this way?

What was the effect on the lives of Peter, Andrew, James, John, and the other disciples of their interest in Jesus? Did following out this interest soften and weaken their lives? Is it only by doing hard, disagreeable tasks that our lives are disciplined? Is there a discipline of higher interest as well as of effort? Did Jesus assign weary tasks as such to discipline his pupils? Think out these answers, and recall present-day discussions about the "soft pedagogy" of interest and the "hard pedagogy" of effort and discipline.

What do you think of this conclusion: The interest of his learners in Jesus led them to make the supreme effort of their lives. As fishermen they would never have expended nervous and muscular energy to the same extent that they did as followers of Jesus. The pedagogy of Jesus was not the soft pedagogy of interest alone nor the hard pedagogy of discipline and effort alone but the combined pedagogy of effort through interest.

In all effective teaching, openers in the form of points of contact must be established between teacher and taught. By a point of contact in teaching we mean how minds come to meet, the common meeting places of mind with mind. Just as we make contact in the physical world, so minds have points of contact in the mental world. Usually these points of contact are matters of common or joint interest. The one who establishes the point of contact knows the other so well or so sympathetically that he identifies with him where he is. To do this involves adaptability and tact on the part of the teacher. He must be thinking about his students as well as about what he himself has to say or do. It is very difficult for a self-conscious or an awkward person to make contacts. He is like a defective electric light bulb: there may be physical contacts but no flashes of light. Can you recall someone who is happy in establishing points of contact? How does he do it?

That such mental meeting places are requisite at the opening of any exchange of ideas is obvious. Without them the hearer may or may not be a party to the transaction. What is said may go over his head or make no real appeal to him. But once two people feel they have common interests, there is a basis for further transactions. Without this sense of contact being established, two minds may pass as ships in the night without speaking. One of the commonest ways of getting together mentally is by a story, incident, or bit of humor. One of the best ways is to play together. What other ways can you think of?

Now, did the master teacher also establish points of contact? Read the following passage carefully and note the answer.

> The next day John was there again with two of his disciples. When he saw Jesus passing by, he said, "Look, the Lamb of God!"
>
> When the two disciples heard him say this, they followed Jesus. Turning around, Jesus saw them following and asked, "What do you want?"
>
> They said, "Rabbi" (which means Teacher), "where are you staying?"
>
> "Come," he replied, "and you will see."
>
> So they went and saw where he was staying, and spent that day with him. It was about the tenth hour.
>
> Andrew, Simon Peter's brother, was one of the two who heard what John had said and who had followed Jesus. This first thing Andrew did was to find his brother Simon and tell him, "We have found the Messiah" (that is, the Christ). And he brought him to Jesus.
>
> Jesus looked at him and said, "You are Simon son of John. You will be called Cephas" (which, when translated, is Peter).
>
> The next day Jesus decided to leave for Galilee. Finding Philip, he said to him, "Follow me."
>
> Philip, like Andrew and Peter, was from the town of Bethsaida. Philip found Nathanael and told him, "We have found the one Moses wrote about in the Law, and about whom the prophets also wrote—Jesus of Nazareth, the son of Joseph."
>
> "Nazareth! Can anything good come from there?" Nathanael asked.

"Come and see," said Philip.

When Jesus saw Nathanael approaching, he said of him, "Here is a true Israelite, in whom there is nothing false."

"How do you know me?" Nathanael asked.

Jesus answered, "I saw you while you were still under the fig tree before Philip called you."

Then Nathanael declared, "Rabbi, you are the Son of God; you are the King of Israel."

Jesus said, "You believe because I told you I saw you under the fig tree. You shall see greater things than that." He then added, "I tell you the truth, you shall see heaven open, and the angels of God ascending and descending on the Son of Man." (John 1:35-51)

As a matter of fact, did Jesus establish contact with the two disciples of the Baptist (Andrew and John), and Peter, and Philip, and Nathanael?

How did he do it? Read the passage again carefully and make a list of your answers.

Now compare your list with the one following.

1. Jesus walked where his presence could be noted by the Baptist.
2. He used his eyes. He observed Andrew and John coming after him, he gazed at Simon, he saw Nathanael approaching and had previously seen him under that fig tree in meditation.
3. He opened up conversation with the two, with Simon, with Philip, and with Nathanael.
4. He asked questions. "What do you want?" "You are Simon, the son of John?" "You believe because I told you I had seen you under that fig tree[?]"
5. He invited companionship. "Come and see." They stayed with him for the rest of that day. "Follow me."
6. He utilized the power of the name. We all like to be recognized and called by name. Further, in mentioning his name, he took a personal liberty in an acceptable way with a sense of humor. "You are Simon son of John. You will be called Cephas."
7. He understood character, and showed that he did. "Here is a true Israelite, in whom there is nothing false." That astonished the doubting Nathanael. The open compliment was not lost on him. His pride was perhaps tickled as he recognized himself under the fine tribute. He began to capitulate. Somewhat bluntly, without

address, he asked: "How do you know me?" The answer, showing
that Jesus had noted him under that fig tree, led to immediate
and unconditional surrender: "Rabbi, you are the Son of God,
you are the King of Israel."

It is little wonder that a teacher who could establish such contacts had
loyal followers. Even so, it is possible that Peter, Andrew, and John were
called again, or even a third time. See Mark 1:16–20 and Luke 5:1–11.
Study these passages. Compare the points of contact. How many different calls to discipleship did Peter receive?

How did Jesus establish a point of contact with the woman of Samaria?
See John 4:1–42, especially verse 8. It was a natural request for a favor. It
was so simple. Yet it surmounted two high walls of separation, that he
was Jew and that she was a Samaritan.

Nicodemus seems to have felt the necessity of establishing a point of
contact with Jesus. How does he do it? See John 3:2. Did Jesus require
such a mode of approach? Do you think Jesus interrupted his speech?
Evidently at some previous time the mind of Nicodemus had opened to
Jesus. How do you imagine it may have come about?

How did the Pharisees and Herodians seek a point of contact with
Jesus? See Matthew 22:16.

The rejection of Jesus in his hometown, "where he had been brought
up," must have been a sorrowful disappointment to him. Was his point
of contact successfully established? What was it? Read very carefully Luke
4:16–30. What caused them to reject him after speaking well of him and
marveling at the gracious words that came from his lips? The point of
contact was the prophecy of Isaiah and its fulfillment.

How did Jesus establish contact with the thirty-eight-year-old invalid
at the pool of Bethesda? See John 5. "Do you want to get well?" is the
question asked on a matter of keenest concern to the man. Find the
question Jesus addressed to the blind men at Jericho.

It is clear that when multitudes followed him it was because effective
points of contact had already been established. Such was the case with
the crowds to whom the Sermon on the Mount was given. The two main
general methods by which he had established such contacts are suggested
in Luke 6:17. What are these? But in the gathering of a crowd there is
another influence at work. What is it? Find it in Matthew 4:24. Putting
these three things together, we see the crowds assembled because of what
Jesus had said and done and because of the spreading of his fame.

Both Matthew and Luke agree that Jesus began the teaching on the hill with the Beatitudes, or characteristics of the blessed life. How did he relate these to something in his hearers' own minds?

On another occasion, when teaching a multitude on the beach as he sat in a boat on the lake, he utilized the parable as the opening point of contact, beginning with that of the sower. How would the parable appeal to something already in the minds of his hearers? Would they be more interested in eternal life or in a story? See Matthew 13. Which appeals to the higher level of interest? Why did Jesus begin his teaching of the multitudes with simple statements and then pass later to figurative language? How did multitudes of people affect Jesus? See Matthew 9:36; 15:32.

Jesus would eat and drink with publicans and sinners. His disciples did the same. This scandalized the Pharisees and their scribes. Why did Jesus do it? See Matthew 9:10-13. What effect did such social freedom have on the Levis and the Magdalenes? Would it be going too far to say Jesus was a good mixer? Does being a good mixer necessitate doing wrong things? Jesus remarked that it was said of him, "Here is a glutton and a drunkard." Why is eating and drinking with a person such an intimate form of contact?

How did Jesus establish contact with Zacchaeus? Read Luke 19:1-10 with this question in mind. How did Jesus meet Zacchaeus more than halfway? How would you describe the habitual attitude of Jesus toward people? Behind every contact established there seems to have been the helpful disposition of Jesus, coupled with the desire to meet the needs of people. How does the incident of Zacchaeus show the use Jesus made of an occasion as it arose?

In the triumphal entry, by riding upon a colt, the foal of a donkey, with what possible content in the minds of the people was Jesus seeking connection? Read Matthew 21:1-11; Mark 11:1-11; Luke 19:29-44; John 12:12-19. Did he succeed? Here an act is used to make an appeal.

After the denial by Peter, how did Jesus reestablish contact with him? See Luke 22:61. Notice the repeated references to the use of his eyes by Jesus. What others can you recall? The resurrection angel sent a special message to Peter. See Mark 16:7. How did Jesus reopen contact with Peter? See John 21:15.

It would be worthwhile to follow this study with a careful account of the contacts Jesus made after the Resurrection with Mary Magdalene in the garden, with Cleopas and John on the way to Emmaus, with the other disciples, and with Thomas.

Sum up now the main modes of contact made by Jesus. How many are there?

By the "motive" of an act what do we mean? You are now doing something. Why? You have in the past undertaken some accomplishment. Why did you do so? Perhaps you are now in the middle of some undertaking, as a student in a school. Why?

We mean two things by motive, either the antecedent reason or the consequent purpose of an act. So the motive is what moves us. We are moved both by an impulse behind the act and by the thought of a result to be accomplished. Thus a man responds to the dinner call. The antecedent reason may be the sensation of hunger or the fear that unless he goes he may be late and miss his meal. The consequent purpose is that he may eat and be satisfied.

May there be action without purpose or end? Certainly all instinctive and involuntary action is of this type. A man sits on a tack and rises in a reflex action. There was an antecedent reason but no consequent purpose nor time to formulate one, though of course there is a desirable result.

Can the two meanings of motive be reduced to one? Perhaps so, in this way: Anything that moves us to act or tends to do so is a motive. But even so, we have to distinguish between sensations and feelings impelling us to action and thoughtful ends voluntarily chosen. In sum, then, a motive is any ground for our action, either a felt antecedent of the act or an anticipated and chosen consequent of the act.

Now, how are teachers concerned with all this? What would you say? Simply this: We get no action from students without first awakening motives. And some motives are more effective and some more desirable than others. To avoid physical pain is a very effective motive. Is it the most desirable motive?

What are some effective motives?

What are some desirable motives?

What is the role of the teacher in motivation? It might be stated in this way: to make the desirable motives effective.

Among effective motives are the avoidance of pain, the securing of pleasure. Among desirable motives are doing right for right's sake, securing the common good, and the like. In certain instances, the effective motive may be desirable, as securing relief from toothache. The desirable motives are also effective, as when for the common good one subordinates his own interest.

The various motives that move people to action are so numerous that it would be well to group them. Could you suggest any way of classifying motives?

We might say that some acts are exclusively for self, some mainly for self and partly for others, some partly for self and mainly for others, and some exclusively for others.

Would you allow that these four classes exist?

If so, we have the following four groups of motives: (1) egoistic, (2) egoistic-altruistic, (3) altruistic-egoistic, and (4) altruistic. As a matter of fact, some deny the existence of the first and fourth groups.

For the average person, which groups of motives are most effective?

Which groups of motives are most desirable?

To what motives did Jesus appeal?

Make a list of these motives.

Classify them according to the four groups given above. What are your results?

In each of the following passages, determine first to what motive Jesus is appealing and second, how this motive should be classified.

The wise and foolish builders, Matthew 7:24–27
Results of belief and unbelief, John 3:16
The sheep and the goats at the judgment, Matthew 25:31–46
Seeking the kingdom of God first, Matthew 6:33
What then shall we have? Mark 10:28–31
True greatness, Matthew 20:21–28
Cross bearing, Matthew 16:24–27
The call of Nathanael, John 1:47–51
The conversation with the Samaritan woman, John 4:4–38
"Fishers of men," Mark 1:16–18
Idle words, Matthew 12:36–37
The unpardonable sin, Mark 3:28–29

What are your conclusions?

To which group of motives did Jesus mainly appeal? How high did he set the standard of motive? How effective were these motives at the time?

How effective have they since proved themselves to be? Is it hard or easy to be a Christian?

Why in the course of twenty centuries has the world not become Christian?

Would you regard the idealism of Jesus as practical?

In speaking of the motives in men to which Jesus appealed, we should distinguish between the motives he intended to arouse and those naturally aroused. Thus some people followed him because they ate of the loaves and were filled, for which they received his rebuke. His intention in feeding them was to relieve their distress, not to secure a following. See John 6:25-27. In the same connection, in removing the lower motive he appealed to a higher motive: "Do not work for food that spoils, but for food that endures to eternal life, which the Son of Man will give you."

We may distinguish not only the egoistic from the altruistic motives but also the natural or intrinsic from the artificial or extrinsic motives or incentives. Can you draw this distinction in advance?

If a pupil works at his algebra because he has to or because he is promised some reward by his parents if he does well in it, then his motive is artificial or extrinsic. If, however, he is interested in it and wants to do it, his motive is natural or intrinsic.

Thus an intrinsic motive is one growing out of the work itself or its natural consequences, while an extrinsic motive is one growing out of some external or arbitrary addition to the thing being done.

Is studying a lesson in order to avoid a penalty an intrinsic or extrinsic motive? Is studying a subject not because one is interested in it but because it is required for admission to college an intrinsic or extrinsic motive? What kind of motive is it if one studies for the sake of the personal development that comes from study?

Review the motives to which Jesus appealed. Are they intrinsic or extrinsic? Are they both? See particularly Mark 10:28-31; 9:43-49.

When are we justified in using extrinsic motives? When not justified? What have maturity and training to do with this matter?

In this connection recall the teaching of Jesus: "A student is not above his teacher, nor a servant above his master. It is enough for the student to be like his teacher, and the servant like his master" (Matthew 10:24-25).

By what motives was Jesus himself animated? Make a list of these motives. How would you classify them? See Mark 1:38; Luke 4:43; John 15:13; Hebrews 12:2; and many other passages.

Would you say that the motives of Jesus were in the third or the fourth class? To draw our conclusions, to what group of motives did Jesus mainly appeal? By which group was he himself mainly moved? Is it possible to act from exclusively altruistic motives?

What may we learn from this study? Shall we appeal to the altruistic and intrinsic motives or to the egoistic and extrinsic?

5

BASIC SKILLS

By learning we frequently mean the interpretation of the new in terms of the old. The familiar or old ideas that we have in mind are what we must use in understanding the new. The old modifies the new, and the new enlarges the old. Thus a reciprocal process goes on between the old and the new, in which, however, the old is usually more influential in modifying the new than the new is in enlarging the old. In those rare cases in which the new displaces the old and itself becomes central in shaping still other incoming new impressions, we have a kind of mental conversion.

So we know by what we have known.

Can you give some examples?

It is only common sense in teaching so to state one's views that they can easily connect with what the class already has in mind. To fail to do so is not to be understood. To do so is to be both interesting and understood. The old Herbartian view was that the new should appeal to the old ideas, and this is still true, but the present view is that the new should appeal to some present felt need or problem.

Can you think of any views stated by Jesus that involve the working of the same principle? Not, of course, that he thought in terms of modern pedagogy.

In this connection recall "He who has ears, let him hear"; "Whoever has will be given more"; "Consider carefully what you hear"; "Let the reader understand"; "Blessed are those who hunger and thirst for righteousness, for they will be filled"; "Therefore every teacher of the law who has been instructed about the kingdom of heaven is like the owner

of a house who brings out of his storeroom new treasures as well as old";
"I came not to abolish . . . , but to fulfill." So he seems to have recognized the working of the principle.

Can you recall instances in his teaching?

Each one of the parables makes use of the more familiar to interpret
the less familiar.

To the woman at the well he speaks of "living water."

To those seeking a sign he refers to the "signs of the times," which
they could not discern, though they could read the weather signs.

When they told him his mother and brothers were standing outside
and would speak to him, he told them who his spiritual mother and
brothers and sisters were.

In justifying his disciples in plucking ears of corn on the Sabbath, he
put their critics in mind of what David did and of what the priests do
on the Sabbath day as the basis for learning what the disciples did.

He puts his synagogue hearers in Nazareth in mind of the messianic
prophecy of Isaiah as the basis for understanding himself (Luke 4:16–30).

Succinctly he presents himself as "the bread of life," as "the light of
the world."

Yet he was not received. John records that he came to his own and his
own did not receive him. He explains it by saying that darkness cannot
understand light. "The light shines in the darkness, but the darkness has
not understood it" (John 1:5). It was a case of failure to perceive. The
main reason was that to the Jews the expected Messiah was a temporal
deliverer, while Jesus taught that his kingdom was spiritual. In vain he
tried to show them that the Messiah was David's lord. They could not
see it. Their mental eyes were blinded by their own assumptions. Even
the disciples after the Resurrection were still earthbound enough to ask:
"Lord, are you at this time going to restore the kingdom to Israel?" (Acts
1:6). So Jerusalem could not recognize the day of its opportunity, the
tragedy of which brought tears from Jesus' eyes.

Perhaps Jesus' recognition of the absence of an attitude of learning is
clearest in his figurative portrayal of why his disciples, unlike John's, did
not fast. The asceticism of John was not the standpoint from which to
understand the festive character of the kingdom. "No one tears a patch
from a new garment and sews it on an old one. If he does, he will have
torn the new garment, and the patch from the new will not match the
old. And no one pours new wine into old wineskins. If he does, the new
wine will burst the skins, the wine will run out and the wineskins will be

ruined. No, new wine must be poured into new wineskins. And no one after drinking old wine wants the new, for he says, 'The old is better'" (Luke 5:36–39).

In this Jesus says plainly that the Baptist is not the basis from which to understand the kingdom.

Jesus desired and labored to be understood by his own people, but it could not be. His thoughts were not their thoughts.

The term *concrete* is usually contrasted with the term *abstract*. What is not concrete is abstract, and what is concrete is not abstract. The table before you is concrete, but the quality of utility that it possesses in common with many other things is abstract.

It is easy to lay down a working line of distinction between the concrete and the abstract. What would you say it is? That which appeals to the senses is concrete, and that which does not appeal to the senses is abstract. Thus individuals are concrete, but the universal human is abstract.

A difficulty arises regarding states of consciousness or some element of a state of consciousness. Is the sensation red, received from looking at a red object, abstract or concrete? The object is, of course, concrete. The sensation is open to inner observation; it appeals to the inner sense. As such it, too, is concrete. Any state of mind studied by introspection is concrete. So our principle holds, whatever appeals to the senses (outer or inner) is concrete.

Now, in the process of learning, which naturally comes first, the concrete or the abstract? The question means, Which naturally appeals more to children, sense reports or thought reports? A series of other questions will bring out the same idea. Which comes first, the particular or the general? the empirical or the rational? the percept or the concept?

Such being the case, let us ask whether we usually illustrate the concrete by the abstract or the abstract by the concrete. Do we use the visible to illustrate the invisible or the invisible to illustrate the visible? For your answer think of the concrete imagery like golden streets, palms, harps, crowns, with which our minds picture the abstract idea, heaven.

How important to the teacher of less mature minds than his own is the art of illustration? What does illustrating the abstract do for it? Does it make it more or less intelligible? vivid? clear?

Concepts without percepts are empty; percepts without concepts are blind. Can you find out what this means? Why is it that a country boy may not be able to see the city for the houses or a city boy the forest for the trees?

The Swiss educational reformer Pestalozzi affirmed that there must be a sense basis for all learning. What did he mean by that? Do you agree with him?

In what region, abstract or concrete, are principles? axioms? theorems? maxims? proverbs? commands? laws? life after death? all moral and religious truths? If these things are to be taught in a realizable way, how is it to be done?

So we come to our question: Did Jesus make use of the concrete in teaching the abstract? As a moral and religious teacher his field was the abstract. His audiences showed various degrees of fitness to follow him. How did he bring abstract truth down to the level of their understanding?

At this point make a list for yourself of all the illustrations of the concrete you can think of in the teachings of Jesus.

Since the concrete is used to help convey the meaning of the abstract, make in a parallel column a corresponding list of the abstract lessons so taught. Do this for yourself first. In doing it you will find perhaps some difficulty in saying at times just what the abstract lesson is, and you may differ from others in interpreting the abstract meaning of the concrete illustrations. This helps to reveal the difficulty of understanding the abstract world. By the way, heaven may be concrete enough to those who are there, but to us now it is, as a place at least, conceived and not perceived, and so it is abstract.

We could ask whether the abstract ideas have objective existence or not, or whether they exist only as features of similarity in particular things, or even whether they are only class names. Does the concrete alone exist?

We might also draw another line of distinction between the concrete and the abstract and say that the concrete is a whole and the abstract is any part of that whole, as a tree is concrete and its leaf is abstract.

Figure 5.1 illustrates how Jesus used the concrete in teaching the abstract. Each separate parable is a study in the concrete.

In addition, every miracle was concrete, but to what extent were the miracles performed to teach abstract lessons? For what purpose were they primarily performed? To relieve suffering or distress or embarrassment? To prove his messiahship?

Further, every event of his life was concrete and has been used by others to teach the abstract, though these events were not so used in every case by himself. What events in his life were used by himself as concrete illustrations of abstract truths? Is this one: "If the head of the house has been called Beelzebub, how much more the members of his household!"?

CONCRETE	ABSTRACT
"Look at the birds" "See . . . the lilies"	Trust
"The wind blows"	The Spirit; action
A little child	True greatness
A poor widow	Genuine benevolence
"Show me a denarius"	Civic duty
"Who is my mother?"	Spiritual kinship
"See this woman?"	True hospitality
"Two sparrows" "Hairs of your head"	Providence
Foxes	Homelessness
Grapes and figs	Fruitful discipleship
"Fishers of men"	Personal work
Things seen and heard	Data for John's judgment
Ox in the ditch Sheep in the pit	Humaneness
Camel and needle's eye	Perils of wealth
The cursed fig tree	Penalty of hypocrisy
Beam and speck	Large and small faults
The narrow way The narrow gate	Difficulty of being good
"Wolves in sheep's clothing"[KJV]	False prophets
"Children of the bridechamber"[KJV]	Festive character of the kingdom
Lifting up eyes to the harvest	Vision of human need
Serpents	Wisdom
Doves	Harmlessness
"Cup of cold water"	Service
"Reed swayed by the wind"	One view of John
Light of the world	?
Salt of the earth	?
A candle in a stand	?
"My yoke"	?
"The face of the sky"	?
The other cheek	?

Fig. 5.1. Jesus used concrete examples to teach abstract concepts.

Fill in for yourself the abstract meaning for the question marks in the second column above.

What additional examples have you of the concrete being used to make plain the abstract?

What now may we as teachers of moral and religious truth learn from the use Jesus made of the concrete?

Suppose you had to teach the lesson of obedience, how would you do it? How did Jesus do it?

In teaching is it better to proceed from the concrete to the abstract, or from the abstract to the concrete? Which did Jesus do in Matthew 6:25-30? Is it from the abstract to the concrete back to the abstract again? How would this question be related to the attainment of students? Is it conceivable that before some people one might proceed from the abstract to the abstract? Would it be desirable?

Which is the bigger mistake, to talk to children in terms of the abstract without the concrete, or to talk to adults in terms of the concrete without the abstract?

In the preparation of the next lesson you have to teach, note its abstract and its concrete elements.

One big practical principle we derive from this study is this: Never try to teach the abstract without attaching it to the concrete. If you have to teach honesty, tell true stories of people who were honest when it was hard to be so.

Is that teaching principle just given abstract or concrete? How would you make it the other?

We have now repeatedly seen how entirely in accord with the best we know today in educational theory is the practice of Jesus. How do you account for this? Would you describe Jesus as a born teacher? Do you think he may have imitated any of his own teachers in the Nazareth synagogue school or elsewhere? Do you suppose he just taught properly in a natural way? Do you think he may ever have considered the methods of teaching in a conscious way? With what problems may he have occupied his mind during the silent years?

The use of symbols is very closely related to the use of the concrete. A symbol is itself something concrete set apart as a design or an emblem to typify the abstract. Acts once performed as well as emblems repeatedly used may both be symbolic. It is a very interesting subject, as we shall find.

Illustrations of symbols may be found in many departments of life. Write down a list of all the symbols that occur to you.

The following is a common set of symbols: + - % # = /

Mathematics and chemistry have long had their symbols for addition, subtraction, multiplication, division, and the common elements and substances.

Is all language symbolic? How about abbreviations? the alphabet? the letter on a college sweater?

Is paper money symbolic? Of what? How about the figures on coins? How about secret codes?

How are gems sometimes used as symbols?

Astronomical and weather symbols abound.

There is a kind of symbolism in which the person treats events not as real but as representing some secret meaning.

We have symbolism in religion. Formal creeds are the best illustrations. Confessions, too, are symbols. Among familiar religious symbols are the cross, the dove, the ox, the lion, and the eagle. Many symbols of the sun are used in both religious and patriotic meanings, as on flags.

Why use symbols? They are a great economy, they appeal to the imagination, they suggest more than can be clearly stated, they are bonds of unity. Think of the signs of the Red Cross, of the YMCA, of fraternity pins, and of insignia on banners and coins.

It is evident that symbols play a large role in religion and in life. There are some who hold that the gospel events themselves are primarily symbols of the common experiences in the life of humanity. Did you ever meet these views? For example, some regard the main events in the life of Jesus as symbolic of agriculture, saying that the first visit to Jerusalem typifies bringing the first fruits into the temple, the baptism is the irrigation of the soil by rain, the temptation shows how grain cannot grow in some soil, the Devil is unfruitfulness, the burial is the death of vegetation in winter, and the Resurrection is the new life of springtime.

How does this impress you? Is there a sense in which the main events in the life of Christ typify what should occur in the life of every Christian?

Did Jesus make use of symbols? Make a list of the possible symbols used by Jesus, and a parallel list of their meanings. Compare it with the symbols and their meanings shown in Figure 5.2.

Here are only six. Ought all these to appear in the list? Have any of these been regarded by some bodies of Christians as realities, not symbols? For example, foot washing and the Eucharist?

Can you think of any proper additions to the list? For example, can

SYMBOL	MEANING
The Lord's Supper	Remembrance of him
The Cross (taking up one's cross)	Sacrifice
Washing the disciples' feet	Humble service
Riding on a donkey on Palm Sunday	Spiritual kingship
"Shake the dust off your feet"	Testimony against
The little child	Humility and trust

**Fig. 5.2. Some symbols and their meanings that
are associated with Christianity.**

the cleansing of the temple be regarded as a symbol of rejection of the sacrificial system?

It is not always easy to distinguish between a symbol and a concrete illustration. The symbol, however, is more or less set apart to render the specific service of recalling its associate. Thus the palm branch is a symbol of victory, and the anchor a symbol of hope. The concrete is any sensible thing. So all symbols are concrete, but not all concrete things are symbols. Thus the ink bottle before me is concrete yet not symbolic. However, an ink pot with a pen is an Egyptian hieroglyph signifying a scribe.

Some of the common symbols for Jesus himself are the good shepherd, the lamb, the lion, and the fish. The reasons for symbolizing Jesus as the good shepherd and the lamb are obvious. The Apocalypse describes Jesus as the lion of the tribe of Judah. The fish is an early Christian symbol of Jesus. The Greek word for fish is *ichthus*, the letters of which are the initials of five Greek words meaning Jesus Christ, Son of God, Savior. The symbol was possibly chosen to throw the persecutors of Christianity off track.

Notice that the remarkable thing about the symbols used by Jesus is that they are acts. Could the baptism of Jesus be regarded as symbolic?

Study Jeremiah 13:1–14 and note the symbol of the belt.

Why are such symbolic acts no longer performed?

Do you see any way to use symbolic acts today?

6

INQUIRY LEARNING

What is a problem? Your answer? What kinds of things lead to inquiries?

When we stand at a fork in the road, we face a problem; that is, in case we are going somewhere and the road is new to us. In such a case our intellectual processes of reflection and inquiry are aroused, leading to a solution of the problem, upon the basis of which we may proceed on our journey.

How many kinds of problems are there?

Some problems grow immediately out of our experience, and their solutions affect daily conduct. These problems are practical in character. Other problems are proposed by the intellect to itself, their solutions are difficult or impossible to reach, and, if reached, they affect life little or none. These problems are theoretical.

Will this distinction between practical and theoretical problems hold? Only in a crude way. A man, let us say, does something wrong and suffers remorse. He may wonder whether he could have done differently. He faces the problem of free will and determination. These are the forks in his road. Is his problem practical or theoretical? We may say practical in the sense that it grows out of his experience and his answer affects his conduct. We may say theoretical in the sense that he is not sure of his answer, which he accepts, not proves.

Can you think of other problems difficult of classification?

How would you classify the problem of life after death? of the existence of God? of spirit communication? of reducing the high cost of living? of increasing the salaries of teachers and preachers? of the Ouija board?

41

In sum, we may say, there are problems whose solutions affect the conduct of life, and these are practical; there are problems whose solutions do not affect the conduct of life, and these are theoretical; and there are problems, like free will, whose solutions are theoretical but whose applications are practical.

Can you see any relationship between the third group of problems and faith? We might say that faith is acting as though a theory were true.

It is also to be observed that the solution of a theoretical problem may in unexpected ways become practical, as when technology helps save life at sea. This is one justification for laboratories of pure research. Another, perhaps, is that knowledge is worth having for its own sake, even if no use can ever be made of it. Is this true?

So, the facing of a problem is the beginning of real thinking. Without a felt difficulty, thinking is only simulated. To think is to think about. And the thing really thought about is the problem. The need of clearing up confusion, of straightening out an ambiguity, of overcoming an obstacle, of covering the gap between things as they are and as they may be when transformed, is, in germ, a problem.

May a problem be present in a situation without being recognized?

Is it a problem in teaching to find the problem?

Is it worthwhile to find the problem first?

Is what the teacher selects as the problem necessarily the same as the student's problem?

May the student have a problem of which he is not aware?

Does the setting of a task necessarily constitute a problem? What does? As a matter of fact, the conditions in experience, the content of life itself, determine whether a matter is or is not a problem and what sort of inquiry it demands.

If facing a felt problem is the beginning of real thinking, it is also the basis of real teaching. Such teaching is not only interesting. It is also effective in changing conduct, and this is what we want in teaching morality and religion, which, if they do not affect life, are nothing.

Did Jesus use the inquiry method? Like all great teachers, Jesus felt that real thinking begins with a problem.

Can you show the truth of this statement?

Can you distinguish between those problems sensed as such by his students and critics and those he brought to their attention? In the latter case they may not have been conscious of their problem until he spoke of it. In which group is Peter's question: "What then will there be for us?" In which group is the teaching of Jesus: "How hard it is to enter the kingdom of God! It is easier for a camel to go through the eye of a needle than for a rich man to enter the kingdom of God"? Were the difficulties raised by his critics real problems?

Shall we say that every person requesting a blessing from Jesus brought a problem with him? Have you a case in mind in which Jesus sensed a deeper problem that was brought? See Mark 2:1–12.

Have you a case in mind in which Jesus declined to deal with the problem brought? In this connection recall the request: "Teacher, tell my brother to divide the inheritance with me." Recall also how he reacted to their desire to make him king.

To realize whether Jesus used the problem method or not, make a list of persons he taught with their problems. To shorten it, you might omit the cases of healing on request, and you might utilize Mark's gospel, as the oldest and the shortest.

After making your list, compare it with the one shown in Figure 6.1.

Doubtless, other incidents in Mark's gospel that contain certain problems could be cited.

Note that the problems faced here by Jesus were mostly not of his own choosing, but were brought to him, sensed as primary by those who brought them. Of three, however, he chose to make an issue, namely, the charge that he had Beelzebub, the indignation at the waste of the ointment, and the conversation of the disciples concerning the greatest.

This study might be carried through the other Gospels. For example, how would you formulate the problem in the mind of Nicodemus as he came to Jesus by night? What were the problems of the woman of Samaria?

Run again through the list given above, and note what solution Jesus gave to each problem and the effects.

The teaching of Jesus shows: problem—solution—action. Shall we regard these three as natural elements of every teaching act?

From the Sermon on the Mount make a list of problems upon which Jesus chose to speak, sensing them as the problems of the multitudes. To what extent, do you suppose, were these problems felt as such by the crowds themselves?

How would you classify the problems upon which Jesus spoke, as practical or theoretical? Which ones, if any, are theoretical?

Did Jesus sense the real needs of men better than they did themselves?

If Jesus had been a teacher of science and philosophy, would he have discussed theoretical problems more?

PERSONS	THEIR PROBLEMS
The scribes, Mark 2:7	Who can forgive sins?
Scribes and Pharisees, Mark 2:16	Jesus' association with sinners
Three groups of disciples, Mark 2:18	Why Jesus' disciples did not fast
The Pharisees, Mark 2:24	Sabbath observance
The scribes, Mark 5:2	How Jesus cast out demons
His fellow townspeople, Mark 6:2-3	Sources of Jesus' power
The scribes and Pharisees, Mark 7:5	Disciples not observing the traditions
The Pharisees, Mark 8:11	They wanted a sign
Peter, James, and John, Mark 9:11	The coming of Elijah
The disciples, Mark 9:34	Who is the greatest?
John and others, Mark 9:38	Tolerance of other workers
The Pharisees, Mark 10:2	Divorce
The rich young ruler, Mark 10:17	Inheriting eternal life
James and John, Mark 10:37	Sitting at the right and left hand
Chief priests, scribes, and elders, Mark 11:28	The authority of Jesus
Pharisees and Herodians, Mark 12:14	The tribute to Caesar
Sadducees, Mark 12:23	The resurrection
A scribe, Mark 12:29	The first commandment
Peter, James, John, and Andrew, Mark 13:4	When shall these things be?
Some at Simon's dinner, Mark 14:4	The waste of ointment
The high priest, Mark 14:61	Did Jesus claim to be the Christ?

Fig. 6.1. Jesus sometimes used the problems people brought to him as opportunities to teach.

What may we as teachers of morality and religion learn from Jesus' use of the problem method?

To what extent does the teaching we know conform to this method?

What would happen if teachers and preachers began with problems?

There is another mode of approach to this matter. The term *problem* suggests particularly something intellectual, though of course problems may be emotional and moral as well as intellectual. The word *need* suggests what is felt as a need.

Make a list of as many as you can of the needs of people that Jesus met.

Compare your list with the following.

The healing of the body
The forgiveness of sin
The release from fear
The satisfaction of the desire to know
The redirection of motive
Relief from Sabbatarianism
Guidance in how to pray
The right valuation of sacrifice and mercy
Social recognition
A universal rule of conduct
A true estimate of wealth
The dignity of humble service
Right regard for children
Ability to be cheerful in a world of tribulation
Knowledge of the greatest commandment
The right attitude toward the letter of Scripture
The increase of faith
The spirit of truth
The resolution of doubt
The showing of the character of his Father
The condemnation of hypocrisy in religion
Ministry to cities and multitudes
The restoration of religious sanity to diseased minds
The satisfaction of hunger
The welcome of sinners

Is there any limit to a list of the needs of the people whom Jesus met?

Could you illustrate from the Gospels each of these needs?

Can you think of any moral or religious need of man not met by Jesus?

Are there needs of men in science, philosophy, art, production, manufacture, commerce, transportation, and politics that are not met by Jesus? In what sense? Would an affirmative answer constitute an unworthy limitation on the influence of Jesus?

To be concrete, may a businessman learn all he needs to know about the psychology of advertising from the Gospels?

Perhaps we must distinguish between the inspiration toward all that is good and needful, which we do find in Jesus, and the attainment of all such useful information, which, of course, we do not find in his recorded words. A Christian may study Greek tragedy, but his Christianity does not tell him what to think of Greek tragedy as a form of art.

We conclude, then, that Jesus met the moral and religious needs of men and inspired them to seek answers to their needs in the abundant life.

What difference would it make in our work if we met people on the grounds of their problems and needs?

7

CONVERSATIONS

The following is a summary of the essentials of good conversation: In politics, in religion, and in the arts of life, opinions are more often changed by friendly talk than by formal speeches. Conversation is not merely a useful art; it is a fine art.

There are two indispensable qualities in a good conversationalist: the first is a good mind, the second is a good heart. The good heart is by far the more important and the one more likely to be disregarded.

A good mind implies (1) natural ability; (2) intelligence; (3) discipline.

A good heart implies (1) good humor; (2) charitableness; (3) candor; (4) sympathy; (5) earnestness; (6) sincerity; (7) modesty.

The good conversationalist is one who can not only talk well but also listen well.

Remember the words of one whose conversations have been the world's most precious legacy for many centuries: "How can you who are evil say anything good? For out of the overflow of the heart the mouth speaks. The good man brings good things out of the good stored up in him, and the evil man brings evil things out of the evil stored up in him." Here we come to the root of the matter. If you would talk well you must live well.

Do the life and words of Jesus reveal the good mind? the good heart? Is there natural ability? intelligence? discipline of mind? good humor? charitableness? candor? sympathy? earnestness? sincerity? modesty?

How would you illustrate each of these characteristics by reference to the conversations of Jesus?

How is the fact that he finally silenced his intellectual critics related to the quality of his mind?

How is the fact that Mary sat with joy at his feet related to the quality of both mind and heart?

How is the fact that he was untrained in the rabbinical schools of the time, yet was able to engage successfully in dialectic with their graduates, related to his natural ability?

How does the conversation concerning the fall of Siloam's tower reveal intelligence?

How does the conversation concerning the baptism of John reveal a well-disciplined mind?

How does the conversation concerning Herod's designs on his life show good humor?

What conversation reveals his charitableness? Was he uncharitable in his conversation with the Pharisees concerning *corban*?

How is his candor revealed in his conversation with Pilate concerning kingship?

How is sympathetic insight shown in his conversation with Martha concerning domestic duties?

Did he ever descend from earnestness to flippancy? How were Peter's words, "You have the words of eternal life," related to the quality of earnestness in Jesus?

How does sincerity appear in his conversation with the rich young ruler concerning inheriting eternal life? Have you further illustrations of sincerity? How do you interpret John 7:8?

How does modesty appear in the conversations of Jesus? Is it in the reply, "Why do you call me good?" Is this trait inconsistent with the self-assertion of Jesus?

Are there other qualities of the good conversationalist? How about fluency? brilliance? wit?

Did Jesus exemplify any of these? Is there caustic wit in his conversation with the Pharisees concerning casting out demons: "Now if I drive out demons by Beelzebub, by whom do your followers drive them out?" (Luke 11:19).

Was Jesus a good listener? How could you show it?

Do you agree with the assertion that Jesus never made speeches?

Almost any book of polite literature dealing with the art of conversation will include such hints as these: don't use slang; avoid exaggeration; be genial; think before you speak; don't argue; exclude religion and politics as topics; conceal temper; don't interrupt the speaker; adapt your conversation to your company; don't correct another in public.

To begin with, did Jesus frequent polite society? Are such conversations recorded? How do the conversations as recorded differ in purpose from those of polite society?

In the days of Socrates, Plato, and Aristotle, men conversed on all the deep interests of life both in public places and in private homes. The results of these conversations were recorded and have since instructed the learned world. How do the conversations of Jesus with his disciples compare with these?

In the list of eleven hints given above, check the ones you think Jesus exemplified. Could you prove your points? Do any figures of speech of Jesus involve exaggeration? Did he argue? Did he discuss religion and politics? Did he at times show feeling in conversation? Have you a clear case where he interrupted a speaker? Did he ever correct the views of others in public? If Jesus had engaged only in polite conversations at such social functions as he attended, should we ever have heard of him? What kind of a guest was he?

Are there still some characteristics of the conversations of Jesus not yet mentioned? Read Mark 10, 11, and 12 with this question in mind.

Can we say that the conversations of Jesus were

1. Brief?
2. Purposeful?
3. Direct, pointed, not evasive?
4. Personal?
5. Making a difference?
6. Instructive, communicative?
7. Accompanied by use of eyes (Mark 10:27)?
8. Responsive?
9. Courageous?
10. Rebuking?
11. Marvelous (Mark 12:17)?
12. Friendly?
13. Appreciative (Mark 12:34)?
14. Pleasure- and pain-giving (Mark 12:37; 10:22)?
15. Monologue or dialogue? Give and take?
16. Quick-witted?
17. Uncompromising?
18. Dignified?
19. Friend- and enemy-making (Mark 12:12)?
20. Stimulating?

Take any one of the conversations of Jesus and find as many qualities in it as you can.

Did Jesus talk shop?

"When in Rome, do as the Romans do." Did Jesus?

Read carefully the following estimate and note any points of disagreement: his sense of humor made the common people hear him gladly. The admonition not to sit in the chief seat at a feast, or ask to dinner only those who will ask you to dine in return, along with the many pithy epigrammatic sayings that the world knows by heart, all show that Jesus was a great conversationalist. He was as witty as he was wise, and he was as ready with pleasantry, satire, ridicule, and irony as he was with invectives.

8

QUESTIONS

In this chapter I sense that we are near the heart of the teaching methods of Jesus.

Recall now as many questions asked by Jesus as you can.

What are some of them?

The four Gospels record more than one hundred different ones.

Here are some of them.

"Why were you searching for me? . . . Didn't you know I had to be in my Father's house?" (his first recorded words, Luke 2:49).

"What do you want?" (John 1:38).

"Dear woman, why do you involve me?" (John 2:4).

"You are Israel's teacher . . . , and do you not understand these things?" (John 3:10).

"I have spoken to you of earthly things and you do not believe; how then will you believe if I speak of heavenly things?" (John 3:12).

"Do you not say, 'Four months more and then the harvest'?" (John 4:35).

"Why are you thinking these things in your hearts? Which is easier: to say, 'Your sins are forgiven,' or to say, 'Get up and walk'?" (Luke 5:22–23).

"Why do you entertain evil thoughts in your hearts?" (Matthew 9:4).

"Do you want to get well?" (John 5:6).

"How can you believe if you accept praise from one another, yet make no effort to obtain the praise that comes from the only God?" (John 5:44).

"But since you do not believe what he wrote, how are you going to believe what I say?" (John 5:47).

"Have you never read what David did when he and his companions were hungry and in need?" (Mark 2:25).

"Or haven't you read in the Law that on the Sabbath the priests in the temple desecrate the day and yet are innocent?" (Matthew 12:5).

"Which is lawful on the Sabbath: to do good or to do evil, to save life or to kill?" (Mark 3:4).

"If any of you has a sheep and it falls into a pit on the Sabbath, will you not take hold of it and lift it out?" (Matthew 12:11).

"But if the salt loses its saltiness, how can it be made salty again?" (Matthew 5:13).

"If you love those who love you, what reward will you get?"(Matthew 5:46).

"Is not life more important than food?" (Matthew 6:25).

"Are you not much more valuable than they?" (Matthew 6:26).

"Who of you by worrying can add a single hour to his life?" (Matthew 6:27).

"And why do you worry about clothes?" (Matthew 6:28).

"Will he not much more clothe you, O you of little faith?" (Matthew 6:30).

"Why do you look at the speck of sawdust in your brother's eye?" (Matthew 7:3).

"Which of you, if his son asks for bread, will give him a stone?" (Matthew 7:9).

"Do people pick grapes from thornbushes, or figs from thistles?" (Matthew 7:16).

"What did you go out into the desert to see?" (Matthew 11:7).

"To what can I compare this generation?" (Matthew 11:16).

"Now which of them will love him more?" (Luke 7:42).

"Do you see this woman?" (Luke 7:44).

"How can Satan drive out Satan?" (Mark 3:23).

"And if I drive out demons by Beelzebub, by whom do your people drive them out?" (Matthew 12:27).

"Or again, how can anyone enter a strong man's house and carry off his possessions unless he first ties up the strong man?" (Matthew 12:29).

"You brood of vipers, how can you who are evil say anything good?" (Matthew 12:34).

"Who is my mother, and who are my brothers?" (Matthew 12:48).

This list is drawn from approximately the first third of the ministry of Jesus. Would it not be worth your while to complete the list?

What are some of the general characteristics of the questions asked by Jesus? Answer for yourself first, and then read on.

A leading question is one in which the very form suggests the answer that is wanted. Did Jesus use leading questions?

Did Socrates make use of leading questions? In honor of Socrates, questioning is sometimes called the Socratic art.

Which is better teaching, to use or not to use leading questions?

Socrates regularly used a long series of leading questions to bring an idea to birth in the mind of his students. Did Jesus do this?

Take the following list of characteristics and find at least one of Jesus' questions illustrating it:

Original
Practical
Personal
Rhetorical
Stimulating
Definite
Searching
Adapted to the individual
Silencing
Clear
Brief

How would you enlarge this list of the characteristics of the questions of Jesus?

Turn to the reason for his questions. For what purposes did Jesus ask questions? Make your own list.

Find at least one question of Jesus used for each of the following purposes.

To make one think.
To secure information for himself (Luke 8:30).
To express an emotion (What emotions are expressed? See John 3:10; Luke 5:22-23; Matthew 12:34).
To introduce a story.
To follow up a story.
To recall the known (Mark 2:25-26).
To awaken conscience.

To elicit faith (Mark 8:29).
To clarify the situation (Mark 10:3).
To rebuke criticism (Mark 2:25-26).
To create a dilemma (Mark 3:4).

Add to this list of purposes.

What are some of the psychological effects of a question?

For example, how does a good question affect understanding? interest? attention? memory? even conduct? To what other psychological effects would you refer?

There were certain questions asked by Jesus that his critics were unable or unwilling to answer. Can you recall some?

Among these were the following.

"I ask you, which is lawful on the Sabbath: to do good or to do evil, to save life or to destroy it?" (Luke 6:9).

"'If one of you has a son or an ox that falls into a well on the Sabbath day, will you not immediately pull him out?' And they had nothing to say" (Luke 14:5-6).

"'John's baptism—where did it come from? Was it from heaven, or from men?' . . . So they answered Jesus, 'We don't know'" (Matthew 21:25, 27).

"'If David then calls him "Lord," how can he be his son?' No one could say a word in reply, and from that day on no one dared to ask him any more questions" (Matthew 22:45-46).

Why did Jesus ask each of these questions?

Can you think of others he asked that they did not answer? Why did they not answer in each case?

If they were unable to answer, why did Jesus decline to answer for them? Pay particular attention to this question. Study Luke 22:67.

How would you answer each of the questions the Jews did not answer, especially the one concerning David's son?

With what manner do you picture Jesus asking questions?

Earnest?
Sympathetic?
Inquisitorial?
Deliberate?
Reproving?
Spontaneous?
Any other manner?

Cite at least one question illustrating each of your answers.

Do you think Jesus ever prepared a question in advance of using it? For example, that concerning the baptism of John, or the Christ as the son of David.

There was at least one question Jesus asked of God. What was it? See Mark 15:34.

How do you interpret this question?

What is its answer?

Does the twenty-second psalm, from which it is a quotation, throw any light on the answer?

Jesus petitioned God for many things. Did he ever ask any other question of God?

From this study do you get the impression that the atmosphere of Jesus was lethargic or charged with intellectual inquiry?

Choosing between these two things, would you say that Jesus came to ask questions or to answer them? Of course he came to do both and did both, but which of these two did he emphasize?

It has been said of Jesus that his aim, as the great teacher, was and ever is not to relieve the reason and conscience of mankind, not to lighten the burden of thought and study, but rather to increase that burden, to make people more conscientious, more eager, more active in mind and moral sense. He came not to answer questions but to ask them; not to settle men's souls but to provoke them; not to save men from problems but to save them from indolence; not to make life easier but to make it more educative.

We are quite in error when we think of Christ as coming to give us a key to life's difficult textbook. He came to give us a finer textbook, calling for keener study, and deeper devotion, and more intelligent and persistent reasoning.

One of the reputed sayings of Jesus is "They who question shall reign." Do you think it sounds like him?

The skillful question is half of knowledge. Do you agree? Can the skillful question be asked without knowledge?

What other phase of the topic, Jesus as questioner, would you like to consider?

How may we become better questioners?

Suppose you were going to talk about asking and answering questions, how would you do it?

Should teachers be as ready to answer questions as to ask them?

What if they don't know the answers?

Which is the more natural situation, when students or teachers ask the questions?

When are questions irrelevant or out of order?

What should the answer to such be?

As we studied the earlier part of the ministry for Jesus' questions, we will study the latter part for his answers, so as not to duplicate material.

First, study for yourself a few of the answers he gave. Note their characteristics. Find them in Matthew 22; Mark 12; and Luke 20.

Let us study some of his answers. After speaking his first parable concerning the four kinds of soils, his disciples asked, "Why do you speak to the people in parables?" See his long, full answer in Matthew 13:10-23. Summarize his answer. Was it satisfactory to the disciples? Is it to you?

Note also that even the disciples did not understand this parable. This seems to have surprised Jesus (Mark 4:13). But at their request he explained its meaning. He made his meaning plain to those who desired it, and he explained why he used parables.

In the midst of the sudden storm that swept down on the lake, they awoke him, saying, "Teacher, don't you care that we drown?" First he quieted the sea and then asked, "Why are you so afraid? Do you still have no faith?"

What is significant in his answer here?

At least three things stand out. First of all he answers the question of alarm by doing something. Then, after quiet was restored and their paroxysm of fear was past, he replied not to their question but to their real need, with two other rhetorical questions in which he rebuked their fearfulness and lack of faith.

At the feast of Matthew Levi, the Pharisees and their scribes murmured against his disciples and asked, "Why does your teacher eat with tax collectors and 'sinners'?" The reply of Jesus was, "It is not the healthy who need a doctor, but the sick. But go and learn what this means: 'I desire mercy, not sacrifice.' For I have not come to call the righteous, but sinners" (Matthew 9:11-13).

Study this answer carefully. Note the figure of speech in the answer. Also the quotation from Hosea. Also the statement of his mission.

Is there any sarcasm in referring to the Pharisees as being well and not needing a physician?

Their question implied a criticism of his conduct. His reply justified his intimate association at table with tax gatherers and sinners.

Some of the disciples of John asked him, "How is it that John's disciples and the disciples of the Pharisees are fasting, but yours are not?" Jesus had the greatest respect for John and his disciples, though their viewpoints of the kingdom were from another era. This question was not asked in criticism. John's disciples were honestly puzzled and wanted light. Jesus replied, "How can the guests of the bridegroom fast while he is with them? They cannot, so long as they have him with them. But the time will come when the bridegroom will be taken from them, and on that day they will fast" (Mark 2:19-20).

What a beautiful figure of speech! Who was the bridegroom?

How gentle a reply! With all tenderness, a full explanation is given as to why his disciples did not fast.

To that part of their question, "Why do we fast?" Jesus did not reply. Is there anything significant in this? Did Jesus want to avoid any criticism of John before his disciples?

Is there tact in this answer?

Why did he refer to the time when his disciples would fast?

In his answer he passes on to give the parable of the new wine and the new cloth. What is the bearing of this parable on the situation? Does it contain by implication the answer to the original question, "Why do we fast"? Note the delicacy of putting the implied criticism of John's system in a parable.

One of his disciples, Andrew, Simon Peter's brother, at the time of the feeding of the five thousand, said to him, "Here is a boy with five small barley loaves and two small fish, but how far will they go among so many?" (John 6:9). "'Bring them here to me,' he said" (Matthew 14:18).

There is a wonderful meaning hidden in this answer to a hopeless question. Think it out.

The whole sixth chapter of John is a rich mine for studying Jesus' answers to questions.

The Pharisees and the scribes asked him, "Why don't your disciples live according to the tradition of the elders instead of eating their food with 'unclean' hands?"

His reply was, "Isaiah was right when he prophesied about you hypocrites; as it is written:

'These people honor me with their lips,
but their hearts are far from me.
They worship me in vain;
their teachings are but rules taught by men.'

You have let go of the commands of God and are holding on to the traditions of men" (Mark 7:5-8).

Does Jesus speak to the Pharisees in the same spirit as he does to John's disciples? What is the difference? Why this difference?

Note that he answers with a question, with a quotation from Isaiah, with an illustration of his charge, and with a parable. Does the fullness of this reply denote any exasperation with the Pharisees?

Compare this answer with that given the Pharisees and Sadducees on seeking a sign. See it in Matthew 16:1-4. Again there is an illustration, a charge, and an Old Testament reference.

Coming down from the Mount of Transfiguration, the disciples asked him, "Why then do the teachers of the law say that Elijah must come first?" And he said, "To be sure, Elijah comes and will restore all things. But I tell you, Elijah has already come, and they did not recognize him, but have done to him everything they wished. In the same way the Son of Man is going to suffer at their hands" (Matthew 17:10-12).

This reply accepts a scribal teaching but gives it a new interpretation. Did Jesus then believe in reincarnation? Who was this Elijah? Did John regard himself as Elijah? See John 1:21. Note the readiness with which Jesus answers questions, even this one involving technical scribal exegesis. How do you explain this?

After his healing of the demoniac boy following the Transfiguration, the disciples came to Jesus and asked him privately, "Why couldn't we drive it out?"

"He replied, 'Because you have so little faith. I tell you the truth, if you have faith as small as a mustard seed, you can say to this mountain, "Move from here to there" and it will move. Nothing will be impossible for you'" (Matthew 17:20). "This kind can come out only by prayer" (Mark 9:29).

What do you see in this answer?

What could Jesus have meant by "faith"?

Are his words to be taken literally? If so, has anyone ever had this faith? If not, what does the figure mean? What kind of a figure is it?

The answer connects faith and prayer. What is the connection in the practice of healing?

These illustrations of the answers of Jesus might be greatly extended. Let us take one more.

The Jews marveled at his teaching given in the temple at the Feast of Tabernacles, saying, "'How did this man get such learning without having studied?' Jesus answered, 'My teaching is not my own. It comes from him who sent me. If anyone chooses to do God's will, he will find out whether my teaching comes from God or whether I speak on my own.'" This was not all he said; see it in John 7:17-19.

Was this an answer at all to the question? If so, what is its meaning? Find and study the replies of Jesus to the following questions.

"Now what do you say?"

"Where is your father?" (Was this intended as a taunt?)

"How can you say that we shall be set free?"

"Aren't we right in saying that you are a Samaritan and demon-possessed?"

"And you have seen Abraham!" (in some translations, "Have you seen Abraham?")

"Lord, how many times shall I forgive my brother when he sins against me?"

"Lord, do you want us to call fire down from heaven to destroy them?"

"Teacher, what good thing must I do to get eternal life?"

"And who is my neighbor?"

"Lord, are you telling this parable to us, or to everyone?"

"Lord, are only a few people going to be saved?"

"Is it lawful for a man to divorce his wife for any and every reason?"

"Why then . . . did Moses command that a man give his wife a certificate of divorce and send her away?"

"What do I still lack?"

"Who then can be saved?"

"What then will there be for us?"

"Lord, don't you care that my sister has left me to do the work by myself?"

"Rabbi, who sinned, this man or his parents, that he was born blind?" (Did the disciples believe that a man's own sin might cause him to be born blind?)

"Who is he, sir? . . . Tell me so that I may believe in him."

"How long will you keep us in suspense?"

"Do you hear what these children are saying?"

"By what authority are you saying these things?"

"Is it right to pay taxes to Caesar or not?"

"Whose wife will she be?"

"Teacher, which is the greatest commandment in the Law?"

"Where do you want us to make preparations for you to eat the Pass-
  over?"
"Lord, are you going to wash my feet?"
"Lord, who is it?"
"Lord, we don't know where you are going, so how can we know the
  way?"
"Is this the way you answer the high priest?"
"Are you the Christ?"
"Are you the king of the Jews?"
"Do you refuse to speak to me?"
"Lord, what about him?"
"Lord, are you at this time going to restore the kingdom to Israel?"

If you have difficulty in finding biblical references for some of these
questions, use a good concordance.
    Ought we to know the Gospels by heart?
    How well do Chinese scholars know Confucius?
    Are you surprised at the number of questions asked of Jesus?
    There are many not in the list given above. Can you add to it?
    Before two questioners Jesus did not answer. Who were these? Why
did he not answer in each case?
    Jesus asked some questions that his critics could not answer. Did they
ever ask him a question he could not answer?
    Was the attitude of Jesus encouraging to questioners? See John 16:19.
    Did Jesus answer the questioner as well as the question? This is one of
the most significant things about his answers. Illustrate from his answer
to the Sadducees concerning the resurrection.
    A good teacher is not only ready to answer but also makes the most of
the answers of his students. Did Jesus do this? In what instances? Recall
such comments as "What you have just said is quite true" and "You are
not far from the kingdom of God."
    It is time to sum up. Draw up a list of the main characteristics of the
answers of Jesus.
    Give at least one answer that illustrates each of the following
characteristics:

    Informational, that is, his answer gave information.
    Profound. For a series of ever more profound answers, see John 6.
    An answer in the form of a question.

An answer in the form of a dilemma.
An answer to the questioner as well as the question.
A real but not obvious answer. See Luke 17:37.
An answer different from the one wanted.
An answer in the form of a story.
Silence in answer.
An indirect answer. See Matthew 18:1-6.
A practical answer to an academic question. See Luke 13:23-24.
Are there still other characteristics of his answers?
Was he ever caught napping?

One of the characteristics of genius is ever to be at one's physical and moral best. Was this true of Jesus?
What may we learn in our own practice from the answers of Jesus? Give some time to this question.

9

DISCOURSES

Under what circumstances is it proper for a teacher to lecture? Think of the right answer to this question.

Is the lecturing that leaves the group passive and impressed justifiable?

Is it proper to lecture on material with which the group is already acquainted?

Is it best to lecture to a small and informal group?

To what extent can you give another person an idea?

"No impression without expression" is an educational principle. How would this principle affect lecturing?

If we could discuss these questions together, we might conclude that lecturing is justifiable when the lecturer has something new to say, when the group is large, too large for question and answer and for discussion, and when the occasion is consequently somewhat formal. But in all these cases, if possible, the lecture should be followed by discussion and conference.

One is sometimes forced into lecturing because of the unpreparedness of the group, though small, to ask, to answer, or to discuss. Are there any such groups! Social habit in any community also has something to do with the passive or active attitude of the listeners.

Can you think of other circumstances under which one should lecture, for example, when immediate information is demanded as a basis of judgment?

Did Jesus ever make use of the lecture method? Preaching is of course one form of this method. The difference probably between an academic lecture and a sermon is that the former appeals mainly to the intellect, while the latter appeals mainly to the emotions and the will; that is, the former communicates ideas, and the latter awakens impulses.

Were the discourses of Jesus academic or practical in character?

It is easy to begin by thinking of the places where Jesus gave his discourses. Recall all you can now. Do this before you read on.

Among these places are the mountain; the lakeside; the synagogue in Nazareth, also in Capernaum and in many other towns and cities; the Mount of Olives, from which the lament over Jerusalem was spoken; Bethesda; in Jerusalem; private homes; the open country; and the temple.

Can you add to this list?

In what place, if any, would Jesus be unwilling to speak?

Think next of the occasions of his discourses. What were some of these?

Among such occasions are the sight of the multitudes; a question asked by one of the crowd; receiving a longer answer than usual; a criticism passed upon some wonderful work of healing done; the sending forth of the Twelve, and also of the seventy; the calumny that he had a devil, requiring refutation; the synagogue service on the Sabbath day; the departure of the messengers of John; the charge that he cast out devils by the prince of devils; the demand for a sign; a question from the disciples, requiring a full answer, concerning, say, the meaning of one of the parables, though only disciples heard such explanations.

Add to this list of occasions when Jesus used the method of public discourse. You will have little difficulty in doing so.

Think about the length of these discourses. Which is the longest one recorded? Where may it be found? How many minutes would it require to read this entire presentation aloud in a deliberate manner? Why not do so and see? (Is it Matthew 5-7 or John 14-17?)

Do you get the impression that the Evangelists give us the full discourse in each case or only portions? See the remarkable statement in John 21:25. Are there instances of their referring to preaching journeys without stating his presentations? See Matthew 4:23. Why do you suppose his discourses were not more fully recorded? Do you suppose that on different occasions Jesus spoke similarly on similar themes?

Do you think the report in Matthew of the Sermon on the Mount, taking about twenty minutes to read aloud deliberately, may be a condensation of what Jesus actually said at greater length? Or may it contain parts of different discourses? For this last question compare Luke 6:20-49 with Matthew 5:3-7:27, noting how much more material Matthew reports than does Luke.

Some think that the discourses of Jesus may have occupied a longer time through his addressing only those near him, say, as he sat on the mountain, and these in turn passing back his words to the others. What do you think of this? Would it be a good method?

To what audiences did Jesus speak publicly? Recall for yourself.

These audiences were differently composed at different times.

Regularly some of the twelve disciples were present, though what makes his discourse public is that others than the twelve disciples heard him at some length on a given theme. These others were at times some of his followers or more or less sympathetic men, women, and children from the neighboring towns or even countries, or at times hostile critics from Jerusalem, or assembled guests at a social dinner. His audiences thus were groups mixed in various ways, from the standpoints of social standing, sex, sympathy with him, and age.

How otherwise would you characterize his audiences?

Would you regard Jesus as a master of assemblies?

By the way, of what church was Jesus the pastor? And to what denomination did he belong? Was he a member of the congregation of a Jewish synagogue? If so, where? Did he cease to be such? If so, when? What difference to us do the answers to such questions make?

Upon what themes did Jesus speak? Or did he rather give expository sermons on Old Testament texts? Did he ever do the latter? See Luke 4:16–22.

Among his themes note the following.

The meaning of the parable of the tares, Matthew 13:36–52
The leaven of the Pharisees, Matthew 16:5–12
His church, Matthew 16:18–20
His coming death, Matthew 16:21–28
His coming death (again), Matthew 17:22–23
His coming death (still again), Matthew 20:17–19
Elijah's coming, Matthew 17:9–13
The mission of the seventy, Luke 10:1–24
Prayer, Luke 11:1–13
The unjust steward, Luke 16:1–13
Occasions of stumbling, Luke 17:1–4
Unprofitable servants, Luke 17:5–10
Faith, Matthew 21:21–22
Humility, John 13:12–20

The Lord's Supper, Matthew 26:26-29
The suffering of the Christ, Luke 24:17-27
The preaching of repentance, Luke 24:36-49
Feeding the lambs and sheep, John 21:15-23
The Great Commission, Matthew 28:16-19

The nineteen discourses listed above are short and were delivered to a portion of the Twelve, or to all the Twelve, or to these with still others of his followers present. These could not strictly be called public discourses, as outsiders did not hear them. Some of these discourses may have been longer than reported.

The following four discourses were delivered to the same chosen groups as above, but are reported at greater length:

The mission of the Twelve, Matthew 10
True greatness, the sinning brother, forgiveness, in one complex discourse, Matthew 18
The Second Coming, the ten virgins, the talents, and the Last Judgment, in one discourse, Matthew 24-25. Compare "all these things," Matthew 26:1.
The farewell discourse and prayer, John 14-17. Is this the longest recorded continuous discourse of Jesus?

Upon the following eight themes he spoke to mixed audiences, apparently small, of disciples and others:

Fasting, Luke 5:33-39
Observance, Matthew 12:1-8
Following him, Luke 9:57-62
Eternal life and the Good Samaritan, Luke 10:25-37
Divorce, Matthew 19:3-12
The peril of wealth, Matthew 19:16-30
The laborers in the vineyard, Matthew 20:1-16
His death and glory, John 12:20-26

Upon the following (how many?) themes he spoke briefly to mixed audiences, apparently large, of disciples and others:

Blasphemy, Matthew 12:22-37

Signs, Matthew 12:38-45
Signs (again), Matthew 16:1-4
Signs (still again) and demons, Luke 11:14-36
Traditions, Matthew 15:1-20
Denunciation of the Pharisees, covetousness, trust, watchfulness, the
    faithful steward, division, and interpreting the time, in one discourse,
    Luke 12
Repentance and the barren fig tree, Luke 13:1-9
The good shepherd, John 10:1-18
His messiahship, John 10:22-38
Sabbath healing, the mustard seed, and leaven, Luke 13:10-21
The elect, Luke 13:23-30
The lament over Jerusalem, Luke 13:34-35
Counting the cost, Luke 14:25-35
The rich man and Lazarus, Luke 16:19-31
The coming of the kingdom, Luke 17:20-37
Prayer, the importunate widow, the Pharisee and publican, Luke 18:1-14
His authority, tribute to Caesar, the resurrection, the great commandment,
    the Son of David, public replies to critics in the temple, Luke 20
Belief and unbelief, John 12:44-45

Upon the following themes he spoke at length to mixed audiences of
disciples and others:

The new kingdom (the Sermon on the Mount), Matthew 5-7
His relations with the Father, John 5:19-47
John the Baptist, Matthew 11:7-30
The first group of parables, Matthew 13:1-53
The second group of parables, Luke 15:1-17:10
The bread of life, John 6:22-65
His mission, John 7-8
Denunciation of Pharisees (his last public discourse?), Matthew 23

Upon the following themes he spoke to others than the disciples; their
presence is not clearly implied:

Forgiveness and the two debtors, Luke 7:36-50
Tradition, Matthew 15:1-20
Denunciation of Pharisees and lawyers, Luke 11:37-54

Modesty, giving feasts, the great supper, and excuses, Luke 14:1-24
Salvation to Zacchaeus, with parable of the pounds, Luke 19:1-27

Reviewing the main themes on which Jesus spoke, what is your impression as to (1) their comprehensiveness; (2) their adaptation to the needs of his day? How many different themes do you estimate there are? Anticipate here the later question: What may we learn from the discourses of Jesus?

Recall also the many references to discourses of his with little or no mention of themes. Compare Matthew 4:17, 23-24; 9:35-38; 11:1; Mark 6:1-6; 11:17; Luke 5:17; 8:1-3; 13:10.

To appreciate both the form and the content of the discourses of Jesus, take one of the longer ones and make an outline of it, indicating the main points.

The following will serve as an example of such an outline. No two outlines made by different persons will be exactly alike. You will note here that in addition to the main points the outline provides an introduction and a conclusion from the record itself and also introduces a summary not in the record. Note whether the outline is strengthened or weakened by these additions.

How would you modify this outline?

Outline of the Sermon on the Mount

I. Introduction: The multitudes, the disciples, the Master, Matthew 4:25; 5:1-2

II. The main points

   A. Beginning: The nine beatitudes: a new set of values, Matthew 5:3-12

   B. Middle

      1. His disciples are salt and light, Matthew 5:13-16

      2. Jesus fulfills the Law and the Prophets, Matthew 5:17-48; five illustrations: murder, adultery, oaths, retaliation, enemies

      3. Righteousness before God, not men, Matthew 6:1-18; three illustrations: almsgiving, prayer, fasting

      4. The true treasure is heavenly, Matthew 6:19-24

      5. Anxiety not for disciples, Matthew 6:25-34

      6. Judgment of others condemned, Matthew 7:1-5

      7. Reverence for sacred things, Matthew 7:6

8. Seeking and finding, Matthew 7:7-11
9. The Golden Rule, Matthew 7:12
10. The two gates, Matthew 7:13-14
11. Warning against false prophets, Matthew 7:15-23
C. Application: The two foundations, Matthew 7:24-27
III. Summary: Jesus sets forth the constitution of the kingdom of heaven
IV. Ending: The multitudes are astonished and follow, Matthew 7:28-8:1

Here is a suggestion about condensing the several main points:
Do they not naturally fall into two big headings? The first part of the material has to do with how Jesus' standard of morality is different from the current. The second part deals with how Jesus' emphasis in religion was different. The Pharisees emphasized the trinity of virtues, almsgiving, prayer, and fasting, and criticized those who did not conform. Jesus insisted upon reality (doing things in secret), charity (judge not that you be not judged), deeds (not everyone who says to me . . .).
Might it not be better to classify this material of eleven points in a couple of big headings?
What do you think of this suggestion?
Thinking over the whole range of the discourses of Jesus, how would you characterize them in a general way?
Are they interesting? profound? original? authoritative? serious? practical? formal? academic? convincing? persuasive? self-conscious? full of variety? monotonous? personal? direct? self-assertive? novel? thoughtful? searching? scientific? artistic? literary? social? moral? spiritual? entertaining? amusing? diverting? simple? uplifting? transforming? intellectual? emotional? truthful? gracious?
Check off in this list of possible characteristics the ones you regard as applicable to the discourses of Jesus. You may want to reread some of them before doing so.
In what manner do you picture Jesus as giving these addresses? It is very difficult to say for sure, for the gospel writers do not portray the addresses of Jesus as a Greek or Roman rhetorician would surely have done. They say next to nothing about his manner. Our own answer must be mainly by means of the imagination.
In particular, as Jesus spoke, was he quiet? impassioned? dignified? enthusiastic? self-forgetful? sympathetic? sensitive to changes in his audience? choked at times with emotion? with or without gestures? with or without flushed countenance and flashing eyes as he denounced the Pharisees? tender? winning? with a natural tone of voice? thrilling?

How else would you describe his manner of presenting truth in discourse?

Do you feel it improper to try to realize the very speaking presence of Jesus in this way? If so, how would you account for this feeling? Would you justify it?

Turn to the effects of his discourses. How did they affect his disciples? the multitudes of common people? the religious leaders? the congregation at the synagogue in Nazareth? those sent by the Pharisees to take him? Why did the common people hear him gladly? Why did his captors testify, "No one ever spoke the way this man does" (John 7:46)? Why did great multitudes follow him after the Sermon on the Mount? What so amazed and angered the group in Nazareth? Why were the Pharisees offended?

Can you recall still other effects of his discourses?

Jesus once said to the disciples who had asked him to explain the parable of the sower: "Don't you understand this parable? How then will you understand any parable?" (Mark 4:13). Does this suggest that he did or did not then have in mind other parables to speak? What does this suggest as to whether Jesus prepared himself in advance for some of his discourses? How are the eighteen silent years related to this question? Undoubtedly much that he said was spoken spontaneously out of a full life. Does this apply to all he said? Recall his promise to the disciples that in the hour of persecution it would be given to them what to say. If you concluded that for certain of his discourses Jesus had prepared himself in advance, would that, in your judgment, detract from him as a teacher?

A topic for investigation: Did Jesus discourse more or converse more? Which do the Evangelists report more, his conversations or his sermons?

We are near the end of our review of this most fertile field of study. Finally, then, what may we learn from Jesus about discourse, lecture, or sermon? Write down as many answers as you can to this question. Look through the preceding material again with this thought in mind. If we, according to our poor ability, would imitate the master teacher in public address, what should we do?

What would be our preparation?

In what places would we be willing to speak?

Before what groups?

Under what circumstances?

Upon what great themes would we speak? Would these themes be problems near to or remote from the lives of those addressed?

Would we repeat the old or herald the new?
In what manner would we speak?
Would we be rather prophets or priests?
Would we trim the truth to suit?
Would we at times antagonize?
Would we "cry aloud, spare not"?[KJV]
What else?

At the conclusion of one of these studies do you get the same impression as the author that there is a great deal more in these topics than we had thought in advance?

Finally, thinking back over the past three chapters, did Jesus prefer to ask questions, to answer questions, or to use the discourse? How can we tell?

10

PARABLES AND MIRACLES

One of the most outstanding features of Jesus as a teacher is that he told stories. We call them parables, though some are not exactly stories but rather short comparisons, as "A city on a hill cannot be hidden" (Matthew 5:14). There are some twenty-eight of these short comparisons and perhaps twenty-five different stories. About one-fourth of all the spoken words of Jesus recorded by Mark are parables in this double sense of the term, and in Luke nearly half. The proportion is largest in Luke. The term *parable* occurs some fifty times in the New Testament.

Some things to do:

Read the four Gospels and make a list of all the short comparisons you can find.

Make another list of the stories.

What proportion of Matthew is occupied by parables?

What do you find peculiar about the form of the parable in John?

Why do you suppose Luke was so attracted by the parables?

What is the nature of a parable?

A parable is a comparison between familiar facts and spiritual truths. This comparison may be short and pithy, like "If a blind man leads a blind man, both will fall into a pit" (Matthew 15:14), or it may be told in a story. If it is told in story form, it may say one thing and mean another, as the story of the lost sheep found by the good shepherd, meaning a lost person found by the Savior (Luke 15:3–7). This is the true form of the parable, or the story may embody in itself the truth taught with-

out referring to another realm beyond itself, as the story of the Good
Samaritan (Luke 10:25-37). This form of the parable may be called an
illustrative story. There is still a third form the story may take. It is one
in which the story and its meaning do not run parallel, like a man and
his shadow, but the two are interwoven with each other, as in the story of
the good shepherd (John 10:1-21).

In summary:

1. Short comparisons, like the three-word shortest parable: "Physician, heal yourself" (Luke 4:23).
2. A story suggesting a comparison between familiar facts and spiritual truths, like the story of the tares in the wheat. This is what people usually mean by a parable. Jesus told the story but not its meaning, unless he was asked to do so privately by his disciples. This kind of parable is familiarly referred to as "an earthly story with a heavenly meaning."
3. An illustrative story carrying the truth within itself, like that of the Pharisee and publican praying in the temple. One might call it a single-story story, not a double-story story, like the group above.
4. Allegory, in which the spiritual meaning of the story is woven into the telling of the story, as in the vine and the branches (John 15). Recall the question raised above as to the peculiar form the parable takes in John's gospel. Can you think of any explanation for this?

Now take your earlier list of the stories told by Jesus, and try to decide
in the case of each story whether it is a true parable, or an illustrative
story, or an allegory.

Which of the three groups is the largest?

What type of mind would prefer the allegory to the parable?

Why not attempt the same with John 10:1-5 and John 6:30-40?

Since the teacher is concerned with the effects of his teaching on the
minds of his pupils, let us ask, What are the mental effects of the parable? This will help us to understand why Jesus made such large use of it.

Try this experiment: Select one of the parables with which you are
least familiar, get someone to read it aloud to you, and note carefully the
mental effects upon yourself. Or you may select a friend and do the same
with that person.

Some of the mental effects of the parable are that it holds attention through interest; it presents a mental challenge to discover the meaning (it is a kind of puzzle one wants to solve); there may be surprise at the turn the story takes; one's personal pride may be touched; it may release effort of will if a personal application is made; and it is an aid to memory. It may give offense if one feels that there is an indirect personal thrust. Compare now your list of effects with this list.

If you would really like to appreciate a parable, stop at this point, and write one yourself.

Why did Jesus use parables?

Before reading further, turn to the following references and try to answer the question for yourself: Matthew 13:10–18, 34–35; Mark 4:10–12, 33–34; Luke 8:9–10.

Now recall that the parables or dark sayings were spoken to a mixed company of enemies and friends, of persons typified by each of the four kinds of soils, and that they were explained privately to the disciples. They were spoken primarily to the indifferent and hostile public, but their spiritual meaning was interpreted only to earnest inquirers.

Why, then, were the parables used? To conceal truth from the unreceptive and to reveal truth to the receptive. The parable was a way of separating the indifferent from the genuine seeker. It was the method whereby Jesus followed his own injunction and did not cast what was holy to the dogs nor his pearls before swine. Had he done so, they would have trampled them under foot (i.e., rejected his plain teaching) and turned against him (i.e., attacked the new prophet) sooner than they finally did. The parable was the word that would judge them at the Last Day, showing that they did not belong to the understanding kind. In repeating the injunction "He who has ears, let him hear," the line of distinction is being drawn between those with and without the hearing ear. So the result was, as the prophet had said, for all their seeing they did not perceive and for all their hearing they did not understand, and so did not turn and receive forgiveness (Matthew 13:14–15).

So we might describe the parables as tests of spiritual insight.

Very likely there are other reasons also why Jesus used the parable. He adopted this method rather suddenly in the middle of his public ministry when the tide of opposition was rising against him, perhaps as a mode of self-protection in his teaching, enabling him to survive until his time should come. Besides, the story is the common oriental method of imparting truth, and the Old Testament prophets (see, for example, Ezekiel 17), as well as the later Jewish rabbis, had used this method though without the perfection of form displayed by Jesus.

Can you think of other reasons why Jesus may have used the parable?

Stop at this point and see whether you understand the parable. State the latent meaning of one of the more difficult parables, for example, equal pay for unequal work (Matthew 20:1–16).

How did the disciples themselves pass this test when they first heard the parables of the sower and the tares?

Not all the sayings of Jesus that go by the name of parables belong in the same class. "Physician, heal yourself" and "If a blind man leads a blind man, both will fall into a pit" are very different from the story of the lost coin, or the lost sheep, or the lost son. These latter say one thing and mean another; they say something about the sense world and mean something about the spiritual world. Both of these differ from the Good Samaritan or the Pharisee and the publican, which combine the spiritual and material worlds in one story. There is no parallelism, but the virtue is embodied in the story itself.

All three of these differ from the good shepherd, in which, as we have seen, the story and the meaning are closely interwoven, and the story is subordinate to the meaning in the telling. Perhaps this last should not be called a parable at all but an allegory. What allegory did John Bunyan write?

The first kind of parable might be called proverbs, maxims, or aphorisms. The second class are properly called parables, because they convey a moral or religious truth in short-story form. The third are illustrative stories. And then, in the fourth place, we have the form that the parables take in John's gospel, the allegory.

Given these four headings, how would you classify

"You cannot serve two masters."
"Take the lowest seat."
The widow and the unjust judge.
The ten virgins.
The tares and the wheat.
The foolish rich man.
The rich man and Lazarus.
The vine and the branches.
The bread of life.

If you want an engaging hunt, classify all the sayings of Jesus you can find that belong under some one of the first three headings. There will be between fifty and seventy-five of them.

But there is a yet more interesting mode of approach to the parables, throwing more light upon the range and quality of the thinking of Jesus. Suppose we classify the parables according to the sphere from which they are drawn, whether things, plants, animals, or people. Some will be difficult to classify according to this principle, for example, the dragnet with the fish, the sower with the seed and the soils, the lost coin with the woman seeking.

What we find on this basis is something like the following.

Things

The salt of the earth
The light of the world
The city set on a hill
The light on a candlestick
Things that defile
Things hidden and revealed
The eye as the light of the body
The new cloth on the old garment
The new wine in the old bottles
The house divided against itself
The two houses built on rock and sand
The four soils
The dragnet
The hidden treasure
The pearl of great price
The great supper

Plants

The budding fig tree
The tree known by its fruits
The barren fig tree
The seed growing independently
The mustard seed
The tares and the wheat
The leaven

Animals

The carcass and the eagles
The children's meat and the dogs

The lost sheep
The sheep and the goats

People
The woman seeking the lost coin
The servants given the talents
The servants given the pounds
The unprofitable servants
Children in the marketplace
The son asking for a fish or an egg
The disciple and his lord
Blind leaders
The two masters
The scribe instructed in the kingdom
The thief in the night
The ten virgins
"Physician, heal yourself"
The whole who need no physician
No fasting in the bridegroom's presence
Counting the cost of war or a tower
The adversary in the way
Guests to take the lowest seat
The neighbor in need of a loaf
The widow and the unjust judge
The unmerciful servant
He to whom much or little is forgiven
The lost son
The two sons commanded to work
The defiant tenants of the vineyard
The unwilling guests
The eleventh-hour man
The Good Samaritan
The Pharisee and the publican
The foolish rich man
The rich man and Lazarus
The unrighteous steward
The faithful steward
Servants looking for their lord

THE PARABLES OF JESUS		
	Number	Percentage
Things	16	26.2
Plants	7	11.5
Animals	4	6.6
People	34	55.7
	61	100.0

Fig. 10.1. The number and percentage of Jesus' parables that can be classified as things, plants, animals, and people.

Where shall we put the parable of the unclean spirit wandering in desert places?

If these classifications are accurate, they show that of a total of sixty-one different parables, sixteen, or about 26 percent, deal with the inanimate world of things, while the remaining 74 percent deal with the animate world of plants, animals, and people (see Fig. 10.1). Of these last, seven, or about 11.5 percent of the total, deal with plants; only four, or some 7 percent, deal with animals; while thirty-four, or over 55 percent, deal with human relations.

Stop here and consider what these results mean for the quality and range of the thinking of Jesus.

It is evident that the thinking of Jesus centered in the human world rather than in the world of animals, plants, and things. This gives a humanistic rather than a realistic or a scientific quality to his thinking. It is also clear from the relatively small place in his thinking of the inanimate world of things that his thinking was not static but dynamic in quality. The phenomena of growth rather than lifeless material especially affected his thinking. And from the great sweep of his illustrations from every department of creation it is clear that Jesus had a wide circle of interests; his thinking was comprehensive and not limited in range.

As pieces of literary composition, would you regard the parables as works of art? As models of the short-story form? Of course, Jesus only spoke them without writing them down, but he spoke them in such a way that they were easily remembered. Besides, he may have thought some of them out carefully in advance. Does not his question, already referred to, when the disciples asked him the meaning of the parable of the sower, perhaps his first parable, "Don't you understand this parable? How then will you understand any parable?" indicate that he had some parables in mind that were not yet spoken?

Now any work of art embodies the ideal in some pleasing form of the real. The parable suggests the poetry of heaven by the prose of earth. It conveys a spiritual meaning by the aid of an earthly story. And this it does in a form pleasing to the imagination. It is proper, then, to regard the parable as a work of art. By the canons of literary criticism, the parable of the prodigal son is the world's greatest short story.

In what does the beauty of this parable consist? Among the most beautiful of the parables are the lost sheep, the lost son, the hidden treasure, and the pearl of great price. Reread these at this point just to enjoy their beauty. Can you find them? If not, use the concordance. You will notice that the first two of these are parables of compassion, the other two are parables of value. Can you feel their beauty?

Now what are the elements of the parable that stir the esthetic sense within us, like a lovely lyric, or a rare sunset, or a beautiful face? It is more important that you should feel the beauty of the parable than that you should understand it. In fact, perhaps the full understanding of it is not accessible to us.

Among the elements of beauty in the parable are economy of expression, not a word too many; and appeal to the imagination, giving us something to see with the mind's eye or hear with the mind's ear. Thus emotions of awe and sublimity are awakened as we envisage that house on the sand wrecked by the storm. There are simplicity and ease of understanding in the familiar part of the parable, and there are profundity and imagination in its recondite meaning. There are harmony between the parts, proportion, and grace, the whole being a unity composed of related parts. There are appropriateness to the occasion and adaptation to the needs of people. The parable is a neat tool, whether it is revealing truth to friends or concealing truth from enemies. It has the beauty of truth, true to nature and to human nature in its divine aspects. In short, like any work of art, the parable is the union of the real and the ideal, the material real with the spiritual ideal. And the union is so full and flawless that we call it beautiful.

Could you illustrate each of these elements in the beauty of a parable? Do you feel their truth? Once again read the following:

"Again, the kingdom of heaven is like a merchant looking for fine pearls. When he found one of great value, he went away and sold everything he had and bought it." Is it not a gem itself?

The parable may be regarded as the analogue of the miracle. This would mean that the parable and the miracle are both alike and unlike. Stop a minute and see whether you can find similarity as well as dissimilarity between the two.

How would it do to say that both the parable and the miracle show the supremacy of the spiritual, but the parable shows it in the region of thought and the miracle in the region of action? In the one case Jesus was expressing his thought, in the other his power.

In this connection recall the unusual miracle of cursing the barren fig tree, unusual because it is the only instance of Jesus' cursing an irresponsible thing. Can we suppose that this miracle was really intended as a parable, that is, as a condemnation of the unfruitful Pharisees? If so, in this instance, instead of speaking the word of the parable, Jesus performed the deed, to suggest spiritual truth. If this interpretation is acceptable, then this incident reveals the close connection between the parable and the miracle. In another connection we should study the use Jesus made of the miracle in his teaching; only a hint of it is given here.

The parables of Jesus suggest to us very interestingly something of his philosophy of life. By the phrase "philosophy of life" we mean one's general view of the world and its effect on conduct; or we might convert the order of these terms and say we mean one's conduct and its effect on a general view of the world.

Jesus saw analogies, comparisons, resemblances everywhere between the realm of matter and the realm of spirit. Thus there were two worlds, but they were related to each other. The first was a type or a symbol of the second. It was less real than the other. It would pass away, but the other would not ("Heaven and earth will pass away, but my words will never pass away"). There is duality of material and spirituality, yet an analogical unity. Nature is a parable of heaven; it means more than it says. The relations of people to the world symbolize the unseen relations of God to his children. This latter is the true and real world, existing now within the heart, and to abide forever.

No doubt you have been wondering whether Jesus originated, or borrowed, or both borrowed and adapted the parable. Read the following:

> The word of the LORD came to me: "Son of man, set your face toward the south; preach against the south and prophesy against the forest of the southland. Say to the southern forest: 'Hear the word of the LORD. This is what the Sovereign LORD says: I am

about to set fire to you, and it will consume all your trees, both green and dry. The blazing flame will not be quenched, and every face from south to north will be scorched by it. Everyone will see that I the LORD have kindled it; it will not be quenched.'"

Then I said, "Ah, Sovereign LORD! They are saying of me, 'Isn't he just telling parables?'" (Ezekiel 20:45–49)

Ezekiel means that Jehovah will use the Babylonians to destroy southern Judea and its capital Jerusalem, as explained plainly in the following chapter. There are many such parables in Ezekiel and in other Old Testament writers, as well as fables, riddles, allegories, proverbs, and the like. For beautiful parables, see 2 Samuel 12:1–9 and 14:1–13. Jesus knew three books, the Old Testament, the book of nature, and the book of life. He found parables in the Old Testament, and he originated parables of nature and of life to set out the new message of the kingdom of heaven. Besides, everybody in the orient tells stories. In sum, we may answer our question by saying that Jesus found, adopted, adapted, and perfected the parable.

This study of the parables could be considerably prolonged, for the subject is rich, and books have been written on it. But, for our purpose, we must conclude now with a few practical suggestions.

It is clear that the art of storytelling should be a part of the teacher's repertory. He should know what the four parts of a story are, should be able to discern these four parts in the parable, should exemplify them in the stories he writes or tells, and should know how to tell stories to a company.

In a book of synonyms or in an unabridged dictionary, find out the differences between parable, allegory, simile, fiction, fable, illustration, and metaphor.

You should also determine your favorite parable as well as discover the favorite parables of your group.

And since the meaning of the parable is its essential part, you should state for yourself the meaning of each of the parables. For example, in the parable of the tares, who sows the good seed? What is the field? What are the good seed? What are the tares? Who sows these? What is the harvest? Who are the reapers? What is the burning of the tares? What is the gathering of the wheat? Jesus himself answers all these questions in explaining the parable to the disciples (Matthew 13:36–43).

Did Jesus intend all the parables to be interpreted in such detail? For example, should we try to say what the two pennies are that the Good Samaritan gave to the innkeeper?

11

USE OF SCRIPTURE

Did Jesus know and use the Scriptures? What Scriptures?
Did he know and use any Scriptures not in our Old Testament?
How did the Jews entitle their Scriptures?
What is the Apocrypha?
Why as a rabbi would Jesus use the Jewish Scriptures?
How is your answer related to the nature of learning?
Make a list of direct quotations from the Old Testament that Jesus used.
This can easily be done by using a New Testament with references or a dictionary of the Bible.
Omitting duplicates, how many direct quotations do you find?
Why is it that some of the quotations do not seem to be exact? Look up "Septuagint."
Compare your list with the following.

1. "Man does not live on bread alone, but on every word that comes from the mouth of God" (Matthew 4:4; Deuteronomy 8:3).
2. "Do not put the Lord your God to the test" (Matthew 4:7; Deuteronomy 6:16).
3. "Worship the Lord your God, and serve him only" (Matthew 4:10; Deuteronomy 6:13).
4. "Do not murder" (Matthew 5:21; Exodus 20:13; Deuteronomy 5:17).
5. "Do not commit adultery" (Matthew 5:27; Exodus 20:14; Deuteronomy 5:18).
6. "Anyone who divorces his wife must give her a certificate of divorce" (Matthew 5:31; Deuteronomy 24:1, 3).

7. "Do not break your oath" (Matthew 5:33; Leviticus 19:12; Numbers 30:2; Deuteronomy 23:21).

8. "Eye for eye, tooth for tooth" (Matthew 5:38; Exodus 21:24; Leviticus 24:20; Deuteronomy 19:21).

9. "Love your neighbor and hate your enemy" (Matthew 5:43; Leviticus 19:18).

10. "I desire mercy, not sacrifice" (Matthew 9:13; 12:7; Hosea 6:6).

11. "I will send my messenger ahead of you" (Matthew 11:10; Malachi 3:1).

12. "You will be ever hearing but never understanding" (Matthew 13:14-15; Isaiah 6:9-10).

13. "Honor your father and mother" (Matthew 15:4; Exodus 20:12; Deuteronomy 5:16).

14. "Anyone who curses his father or mother must be put to death" (Matthew 15:4; Exodus 21:17; Leviticus 20:9).

15. "These people honor me with their lips" (Matthew 15:8-9; Isaiah 29:13).

16. "At the beginning the Creator 'made them male and female'" (Matthew 19:4; Genesis 1:27; 5:2).

17. "For this reason a man will leave his father and mother and be united to his wife" (Matthew 19:5; Genesis 2:24).

18. "'Do not murder, do not commit adultery, do not steal, do not give false testimony, honor your father and mother,' and 'love your neighbor as yourself'" (Matthew 19:18-19; Exodus 20:12-16; Deuteronomy 5:16-20).

19. "'From the lips of children and infants you have ordained praise'" (Matthew 21:16; Psalm 8:2).

20. "'The stone the builders rejected has become the capstone'" (Matthew 21:42; Psalm 118:22).

21. "'My house will be called a house of prayer,' but you are making it a 'den of robbers'" (Matthew 21:13; Isaiah 56:7; Jeremiah 7:11).

22. "'I am the God of Abraham, the God of Isaac, and the God of Jacob'" (Matthew 22:32; Exodus 3:6).

23. "'Love the Lord your God with all your heart and with all your soul and with all your mind'" (Matthew 22:37; Deuteronomy 6:5).

24. "'Love your neighbor as yourself'" (Matthew 22:39; Leviticus 19:18).

25. "'The Lord said to my Lord: "Sit at my right hand until I put your enemies under your feet"'" (Matthew 22:44; Psalm 110:1).

26. "'I will strike the shepherd, and the sheep of the flock will be scattered'" (Matthew 26:31; Zechariah 13:7).

27. *"Eloi, Eloi, lama sabachthani?"* (Matthew 27:46; Psalm 22:1).
28. "'And he was numbered with the transgressors'" (Luke 22:37; Isaiah 53:12).
29. "Father, into your hands I commit my spirit" (Luke 23:46; Psalm 31:5).
30. "The Spirit of the Lord is on me" (Luke 4:18; Isaiah 61:1-2).
31. "'I have said you are gods'" (John 10:34; Psalm 82:6).
32. "'He who shares my bread has lifted up his heel against me'" (John 13:18; Psalm 41:9).
33. "'They hated me without reason'" (John 15:25; Psalm 35:19; Psalm 69:4).

This list is not complete.

What impression do you get as to the familiarity of Jesus with the letter of Scripture?

From what portions of the Scriptures does he quote most?

Upon what occasions in his life does he draw upon Scripture? For example, the temptation? the first sermon in Nazareth? the Sermon on the Mount? in meeting criticism? in answering questions? in asking questions? in his relation to John? in his explanation of the use of parables? in cleansing the temple? in announcing his death? in announcing the betrayal? in explaining opposition? on the cross?

How did he regard his own teaching, life, and death as related to Scripture? See John 5:9, 40.

Is it likely that we have all the quotations he made from Scripture? In answering a question like this, recall that some scholars say that all the incidents reported in the Gospels fall on only thirty-five different days throughout a period of some three years. See also the remarkable last verse in the gospel of John.

Also take this little problem in arithmetic. One-third of the gospel of John is devoted to one week in the life of Christ. Suppose all his weeks during three years of public ministry had been equally full and equally fully reported; how many gospels the length of John's would have been necessary?

Did Jesus ever write out any of his teaching for preservation? Why not?

Upon what principle did some of his words survive?

How did he obtain this intimacy with Scripture? When?

What is his attitude toward Scripture in the Sermon on the Mount? Did he accept it as final authority?

Continue this study by making a list of his references and allusions to the Old Testament without directly quoting it. This can be done by reading through one Gospel with this thought in mind.

What will such a list show?

Compare your list with the following.

1. The persecution of the prophets, Matthew 5:12
2. The gift that Moses commanded, Matthew 8:4
3. Those who will sit down with Abraham, Isaac, and Jacob in the kingdom of heaven, Matthew 8:11
4. Sodom and Gomorrah in the judgment, Matthew 10:15
5. "Elijah has already come," Matthew 17:12; 11:14
6. A man's foes (cf. Micah 7:6), Matthew 10:36
7. What David did, Matthew 12:3
8. How the priests profane the Sabbath, Matthew 12:5
9. Jonah and Nineveh, Matthew 12:40–41
10. The Queen of the South, Matthew 12:42
11. The blood of Abel, Matthew 23:35
12. The days of Noah, Matthew 24:37
13. The mourning of the tribes of the earth, Matthew 24:30
14. The sign of the Son of Man in heaven, Matthew 24:30
15. Sitting at the right hand of power, Matthew 26:64
16. The widows in Israel, Luke 4:25
17. The lepers in Israel, Luke 4:27
18. The days of Lot, Luke 17:28
19. Lot's wife, Luke 17:32
20. Searching the Scriptures, John 5:39
21. Moses "wrote about me," John 5:46
22. The witness of two, John 8:17
23. Ascending and descending angels, John 1:51
24. Lifting up the serpent, John 3:14
25. The bondservant in the house, John 8:35
26. The rejoicing of Abraham, John 8:56

You can easily identify these Old Testament allusions by using a reference Bible on the passages given. This list is not exhaustive.

You can also test your familiarity with the Old Testament by noting how many you need to look up.

How do you think your knowledge of the Old Testament compares with that which Jesus showed?

What do these allusions show as to the ability of Jesus to use the Old Testament? Was he bound by its letter? He evidently used its incidents freely and independently of the words reporting them.

There are some references by Jesus to what had been written that cannot be identified. Do you know of any?

Here is a partial list.

1. "The Son of Man will go just as it is written about him." (Where?) Matthew 26:24
2. "But how then would the Scriptures be fulfilled that say it must happen in this way?" (What Scriptures?) Matthew 26:54
3. "But this has all taken place that the writings of the prophets might be fulfilled." (What prophets?) Matthew 26:56
4. "But I tell you, Elijah has come, and they have done to him everything they wished, just as it is written about him." (Where?) Mark 9:13
5. "Because of this, God in his wisdom said, 'I will send them prophets and apostles, some of whom they will kill and others they will persecute.'" (Where? What is the wisdom of God?) Luke 11:49
6. "For this is the time of punishment in fulfillment of all that has been written." (What things?) Luke 21:22
7. "Whoever believes in me, as the Scripture has said, streams of living water will flow from within him." John 7:38; compare Isaiah 12:3 and Ezekiel 47:1
8. "None has been lost except the one doomed to destruction so that Scripture would be fulfilled." (What Scripture?) John 17:12

There are other passages of this kind. How do you explain them?

Was Jesus here referring to the general tenor and spirit of the Scriptures?

Is it conceivable that he may have referred to what was written in the mind of God?

Did Jesus tend to regard what had happened as the fulfillment of Scripture even when specific references are lacking?

Would such an attitude of mind make the endurance of suffering easier?

What do such passages indicate as to the reliance of Jesus on Scripture? as to the way in which the thought of Scripture filled his mind?

There is such a thing as knowing the Bible so well that one's literary or spoken style unconsciously reflects its form of expression.

Is it possible, similarly, that Jesus may have used Old Testament forms of expression naturally, without intending to quote?

In the light of this question study the following pairs of quotations:

1. "Blessed are those who mourn, for they will be comforted." Matthew 5:4
   "To comfort all who mourn." Isaiah 61:2
2. "Blessed are the meek, for they will inherit the earth." Matthew 5:5
   "The meek will inherit the land." Psalm 37:11
3. "Blessed are the pure in heart, for they will see God." Matthew 5:8
   "He who has clean hands and a pure heart." Psalm 24:4
4. "Either by heaven, for it is God's throne; or by the earth, for it is his footstool." Matthew 5:34–35
   "Heaven is my throne and the earth is my footstool." Isaiah 66:1
5. "Seek and you will find." Matthew 7:7
   "If you seek him, he will be found by you." 1 Chronicles 28:9

There are about forty similar parallel passages.

What conclusion do you draw?

We have seen quotations, and allusions, and similar literary form connecting the teaching of Jesus with the Scriptures.

A more profound line of inquiry would be to ask how his thinking is related to Old Testament thinking.

Are the matters that he makes fundamental also to be found in the Old Testament? God as father? See Psalm 103:13. Love of God and neighbor? The kingdom of God? See Daniel 2:44; 7:27.

With this thought in mind, compare the following passages:

"The Sabbath was made for man, not man for the Sabbath." Mark 2:27

"No one can enter the kingdom of God unless he is born of water and the Spirit." John 3:5

"Six days do your work, but on the seventh day do not work." Exodus 23:12

"I will sprinkle clean water on you, and you will be clean. . . . I will . . . put a new spirit in you." Ezekiel 36:25–26

But is there any real Old Testament parallel for Matthew 5:44: "Love your enemies"? Compare Job 31:29–30; Psalm 7:4; Exodus 23:4.

Still another question. The Jews had religious writings that do not appear in our Old Testament, known as the Apocrypha. Was Jesus acquainted with these writings also?

Read the following passages and decide for yourself.

"Do not inure your mouth to oaths or make a habit of naming the Holy One." Ecclesiasticus 23:9 (Cf. Matt. 5:34–35)

"Do not reject the appeal of a man in distress or turn your back on the poor; when he begs for alms, do not look the other way and so give him reason to curse you." Ecclesiasticus 4:4–5 (Cf. Matt. 5:42)

"Lend to your neighbour in his time of his need; repay your neighbour punctually." Ecclesiasticus 29:2 (Cf. Matt. 5:42)

"Forgive your neighbour his wrongdoing; then, when you pray, your sins will be forgiven." Ecclesiasticus 28:2 (Cf. Matt. 6:12, 14). The book of Ecclesiasticus or The Wisdom of Jesus the Son of Sirach was probably written 100–50 B.C. It resembles the Proverbs, is probably superior to Proverbs in moral quality, and may be read with edification.

"You taught your people by such works as these, how that the righteous must be a lover of men." The Wisdom of Solomon, circa 100 B.C.

"And what you admire, give to others." Tobit 4:15; compare Matthew 7:12. Tobit, like Confucius, gives the golden rule in negative form.

What is your conclusion as to whether Jesus knew the Apocrypha?

Jesus does not quote directly from the Apocrypha in what has come down to us, but it is evident his thoughts are similar.

Should we then study the Apocrypha? (The Apocrypha was written in Greek and Latin. It contains fourteen books. The original meaning of the term is "hidden." In the second century the meaning changed to "spurious." The titles of the fourteen books are: 1 and 2 Esdras, Tobit, Judith, The Remainder of Esther, The Wisdom of Solomon, Ecclesiasticus, Baruch, Song of the Three Holy Children, History of Susanna, Bel and the Dragon, Prayer of Manasseh, and 1 and 2 Maccabees. These books are accepted as canonical, that is, "genuine and inspired," by the Roman Catholic Church but are rejected by the Jews and the Protestant churches. Are writings or writers inspired? May inspiration be received from a writing not accepted as "inspired"?)

Let us turn briefly to the next question: What was Jesus' relationship to the Scriptures of his day?

Original he was, else we should never have had a "New" Testament.

How do you answer the question?

In the following list of statements, check off the ones with which you agree.

Jesus was original in teaching the love of enemies.

He was original in selection and emphasis; that is, out of a mass of Old Testament views he selected certain ones for primary emphasis.

He was original in clarifying, amplifying, and applying the views selected. (How many times is God referred to as "Father" in the Old Testament and in the New?)

He was original in substituting the spirit of love, which fulfills law naturally, for the law itself and its letter.

He was original and unique in living what he taught.

He was original and unique in his personal claim to fulfill Scripture, to be the Messiah. Jesus' becoming and being Christ is the new thing.

He is original in the universality of his vision, coupled with the individuality, not nationality, of his appeal.

He is original as is an artist who sits in the presence of the greatest of his predecessors, assimilating and absorbing until he comes into his own creative self-expression.

He is original and unique in being a nonracial man, that is, realizing the moral and religious capacities of all humanity.

He is original and unique in his unbroken sense of union and communion with God.

With which statements are you not in agreement?

What statement of his originality would you add?

What other religion besides Christianity has ever bound up with its own sacred writings those of another religion? What is the significance of this fact?

Summarizing our study of how Jesus used Scripture, let me append certain statements of scholars. Check the ones with which you agree.

"The mind of Jesus was saturated with the Book of Isaiah."

"Jesus was an authoritative interpreter of the Old Testament."

"He had so absorbed the Old Testament that its ideals were his commonplaces of thought."

"Jesus joined the work which he did as closely as possible to that of the Old Testament prophets, using their authority for his teachings."

"Jesus was also a prophet greater than any that had gone before him."

"The great ideas that were regulative of the Old Testament revelation were also those which guided the practice and conduct of our Lord" (compare Matthew 3:15).

"The body of his teaching is everywhere permeated by Old Testament ideas and colored by Old Testament language."

"He subjected himself to its spiritual authority."

"Jesus recognized the process of evolution that took place in Old Testament revelation" (compare his setting aside certain precepts of the law and his reference to Tyre and Sidon).

"Jesus used the Old Testament as the source of his own life."

"The Old Testament presents to us characters that are supremely worthy of our reverence because they were consciously centered in God and full of his power. It permits us to share the enthusiasm of the men who knew the fundamentals of our religion and the character of our God. It is indispensable to complete discipleship of Christ, because it is the creator of the mould into which his soul expanded."

"Higher values than these, religiously, there are not."

Why is the Old Testament "old"? Who made it so?

Is the New Testament still "new"? Will it ever become "old"?

Some Final Practicalities

Jesus used the Old Testament for the growth of his own soul. Do we need it for the same?

He also used it as the common meeting ground with the religious minds of his day. What analogous use should we make of it?

What should be the attitude of Christianity toward the Jewish religion today? of Christians toward Jews?

What should be the attitude of the missionary toward the religion and the religious writings of the people to whom he goes?

Can a Christian understand the mind of Christ without understanding Moses and Elijah, the Law and the Prophets? Recall the Transfiguration.

What does this study mean to you personally? That the moral and religious teacher should be a student of religious literature? Especially of religious literature of the highest inspirational value?

Such acquisition will enter into the fiber of his own personality, will affect the quality of his speech and conversation, and will become the basis of his conscious and unconscious appeal to others. It would even be profitable to study the world's religious literature comparatively and read some of the sacred writings of the Hindus, Persians, Chinese, and Arabs. In consequence, biblical literature would mean not less but more.

Do we know enough?

What are we going to do about it?

12

TEACHABLE MOMENTS

Leading educational thinkers are saying today that education must be vital, must grow out of a situation, must satisfy a felt need, must solve a real problem. In this way the ideas gained begin to function at once. All this means that education must be in immediate contact with actual living and so not formal, not academic, not only for its own sake.

Can you restate the viewpoint of the preceding paragraph in your own language?

Do you find yourself in agreement?

Would you say that Jesus assigned to the apostles a task in which they were interested but which required further thought before its completion? What was that task?

Can you now foresee what is coming in our discussion of the use Jesus made of the natural occasion as it arose?

Do we really learn more in or out of school? Why?

What difference does it make in your study whether you have a purpose or not?

At this point recall one natural occasion arising in the life of Jesus and the use he made of it to do or say something worthwhile. Some further illustrations of the same are listed in Figure 12.1.

This list covers about one-fourth of the illustrations the Gospels provide. Perhaps they are enough to illustrate adequately the point that it was characteristic of Jesus to make use of the occasion as it arose. This is one of the reasons for the vitality of his teaching.

Make a supplementary list for yourself of the natural occasions Jesus used as they arose and the use he made of them either in action or speech.

THE OCCASION	ITS USE
Finding the traders in the temple	Cleaning the temple
Nicodemus came to him	Teaching the birth from above
There came a woman of Samaria	Transforming a life
The leper came to him	Cleaning physical life
The bringing of the palsied man	Spiritual and physical healing
He saw a man lying at the pool of Bethesda	Physical healing
The murmuring of the Pharisees at the disciples for plucking ears of corn on the Sabbath	Teaching about the Sabbath
Seeing the multitudes	Sermon on the Mount
The coming of John's messengers	A message to John
Eating with Simon the Pharisee	Parable of the two debtors
The charge: "This man has Beelzebub"	The unpardonable sin
The coming of his mother and brothers	Supremacy of spiritual relations
The disciples' question, "Why do you speak to them in parables?"	Mysteries of the kingdom
The disciples request an explanation for the parable of the tares	The sons of evil
"Why does your master eat with publicans?"	The well and the sick

Fig. 12.1. Jesus utilized "teachable moments."

Doing this will bring home to you the meaning of the use of teachable moments.

Can you imagine Jesus letting an occasion slip?

Is it customary for us to use the occasion or let it slip? Why do we do so?

What has the lack of courage and the lack of power to do with it?

What kind of a guest was Jesus, for example, in the home of Simon the Pharisee or of Martha and Mary?

Was the personality of Jesus so dominating that he simply mastered every occasion, or do you think of him at times as merging his personality in that of the company, as, say, at the wedding in Cana?

Did Jesus ever make formal engagements in advance to appear at a certain place at a given time to heal, or teach, or preach?

Shall we conclude that the only kind of teaching Jesus did was occasional in character? If so, we must not neglect to add that he himself, being who he was, had much to do with causing these occasions to arise. Also, that he specifically created certain occasions, as when, having heard that the Pharisees had excommunicated the healed man born blind, Jesus sought him out and ministered to him (John 9:35).

Can you think of other occasions that Jesus created?

Which is the greater opportunity for the teacher, the lesson in manners and morals or some good or bad act in school?

What difference would it make if we began now to use teachable moments rather than the formal occasions?

13

WORD PICTURES

Run down the following list of words with your eye and think the corresponding opposite in each case.

Good
Light
True
Black
Old
Summer
Positive
Beautiful
Health
Spiritual
God

Did it require much time to do so?

Write the opposites in a parallel column.

This is one form of association of ideas, that of contrast. You notice how natural and easy it is to have associations of this kind. Make a list of other pairs of opposites.

What are some of the effects of the use of contrast? Think of its use in art, in handling forms and colors.

Placing opposites over against each other reveals differences between members of a single group, exhibits the dissimilar qualities in the things compared, emphasizes their opposite nature, has a pictorial quality and so appeals to the imagination, and is likewise an aid to attention and memory.

For all these reasons the use of contrast is a great aid in the art of teaching.

Did Jesus make use of the principle of contrast in his teaching? Make a list of illustrations involving contrast. Usually these illustrations are most obvious where the contrast is between just two persons, but often the contrast appears also in a more complex situation.

As used by Jesus the contrast is not introduced primarily for artistic purposes but for didactic purposes. Still, its use so heightens the effect that artists readily spread such scenes on canvas, as, say, the two men in the temple, or the Last Judgment.

Let us study the following illustrations of contrast.

1. Lesson: the fulfilling of the law.
   Formula of contrast: "You have heard . . . but I tell you."
   These contrasts appear, of course, in the Sermon on the Mount.
   How many times is the formula repeated? See Matthew 5:21-22, 27-28, 33-34, 38-39, 43-44.

2. Lesson: sincerity in religion.
   Contrast: The hypocrites and Jesus' disciples.
   These contrasts likewise appear in the Sermon on the Mount.
   How many times is this contrast made? See Matthew 6:2-4, 5-15, 16-18.
   Study the use of the word *but* in the following passages: Matthew 5:22, 28, 34, 39, 44; 6:3, 6, 17. What is its effect?

3. Lesson: God the common Father of all.
   Contrasts: the one lost sheep and the ninety-nine.
   The one lost coin and the nine.
   The one lost son and the older brother. See Luke 15.
   What social classes are typified by the two sides of the contrast?

4. Lesson: true obedience.
   Contrast: the two sons commanded to work in the vineyard: Matthew 21:28-32.
   Who are these two sons?

5. Lesson: true treasure.
   Contrast: treasure on earth and in heaven: Matthew 6:19-21.
   What two classes are here intended?
6. Lesson: watchfulness.
   Contrast: wise and foolish virgins: Matthew 25:1-13.
   What new feature of contrast appears in this illustration?

7. Lesson: the final separation of good and bad.
   Contrast: the sheep and the goats: Matthew 25:31-40.
   How large are the contrasted groups in the illustration?

8. Lesson: the real neighbor.
   Contrast the priest, the Levite, and the Good Samaritan: Luke
      10:25-37.
   What variation in the use of contrast appears here?

In the same way find the lesson taught and the contrast used in each of
the following passages: Matthew 5:17-20; 7:24-27; 18:21-35; Luke 12:4-5,
8-9, 10; 18:9-14; John 4:13-14, 21-22.

How is the principle of contrast as used in the parable of the talents
and the pounds like, and also unlike, that in the parable of the Good
Samaritan?

How does contrast appear in the parable of the sower? in the parable
of the rich man and Lazarus? in the directions concerning whom to in-
vite to a supper?

Note that in the parable of the prodigal son the contrast is, as usual,
between one and one; in the parable of the Good Samaritan between one
and two; in the parable of the talents and pounds between two and one;
in the parable of the sower between one and three kinds of soil; in the
parable of the lost coin between one and nine; in the parable of the lost
sheep between one and ninety-nine; in the parable of the virgins between
five and five; and in the portrayal of the Last Judgment between two
great groups embracing all. Have you still other variations to note?

Perhaps there is no phase of the method used by Jesus as a teacher
that more clearly shows its esthetic quality than this of contrast. It reveals his feeling for the form of spoken discourse, as a part of one's effec-
tiveness in presenting ideas.

If you were teaching the lesson of honesty to a group and wanted to
use the principle of contrast, how would you do it?

What is the danger in telling young people about dishonest children?

Dealing in likenesses, contrasts, and suggestions, figures flash word pictures that vitalize all language, spoken or written, from conversation to poetry.

The most forceful figures are consequently those based on imagery: simile, metaphor, personification, and irony.

In addition to these, there are allusion, allegory, parable, and hyperbole. This gives us a list of figures of speech.

Now let us see what will happen if we inquire which of these figures Jesus used.

Simile. As the word, from the Latin, suggests, a simile says one thing is like another. "How often I have longed to gather your children together, as a hen gathers her chicks under her wings, but you were not willing" (Matthew 23:37).

Metaphor. The metaphor is an abbreviated simile, omitting the word of comparison. "Go tell that fox" (Herod; Luke 13:32).

Personification. This figure endows things with personality: "The wind blows wherever it pleases" (John 3:8).

Irony. In this figure one means the opposite of what the words say: "You have a fine way of setting aside the commands of God in order to observe your own traditions!" (Mark 7:9).

Allusion. This figure is an indirect reference: "Destroy this temple, and I will raise it again in three days" (John 2:19).

Allegory. This figure is a sustained metaphor or simile: "I am the vine, you are the branches" (John 15:5; see vv. 1–10).

Parable. A brief story with a moral or religious meaning: the sower, the Good Samaritan.

Hyperbole, or rhetorical overstatement: "You blind guides! You strain out a gnat but swallow a camel" (Matthew 23:24).

Thus we have found in the recorded words of Jesus examples of many of the figures of speech used by modern authors.

What impression do you gain from this fact?

Can you give additional illustrations of each of the figures so far discussed?

Let us turn to still other figures or forms of speech. I am not so particular that you should be able to name these as that you should feel their quality and sense the addition they make to spoken style.

"Come, follow me, . . . and I will make you fishers of men" (Matthew 4:19).

"Let the dead bury their own dead" (Matthew 8:22).

"So the last will be first, and the first will be last" (Matthew 20:16).

"For whoever wants to save his life will lose it, but whoever loses his life for me and for the gosepl will save it" (Mark 8:35).

"It is easier for a camel to go through the eye of a needle than for a rich man to enter the kingdom of God" (Mark 10:25).

"You know how to interpret the appearance of the sky, but you cannot interpret the signs of the times" (Matthew 16:3).

"And I tell you that you are Peter [a stone], and on this rock I will build my church, and the gates of Hades will not overcome it" (Matthew 16:18). What is the meaning of this?

"Those who exercise authority over them [the Gentiles] call themselves Benefactors" (Luke 22:25).

"If a house is divided against itself, that house cannot stand" (Mark 3:25).

"You hear with one ear, but the other one has been closed" (reputed saying).

"Can a blind man lead a blind man?" (Luke 6:39).

"The rich man also died and was buried" (Luke 16:22).

"Neither do people light a lamp and put it under a bowl" (Matthew 5:15). This saying of our Lord is as picturesque as it is forceful. It gives us a glimpse into a Galilean home, where the commonest articles of furniture would be the lamp, the lampstand, the seah measure, and the couch. And who could fail to apprehend the force of the metaphor?

"First take the plank out of your own eye" (Matthew 7:5).

"Do not give dogs what is sacred" (Matthew 7:6).

"Do people pick grapes from thornbushes?" (Matthew 7:16).

"If he asks for an egg, will [you] give him a scorpion?" (Luke 11:12).

"You snakes! You brood of vipers! How will you escape being condemned to hell?" (Matthew 23:33).

"It is not the healthy who need a doctor" (Mark 2:17).

"I have shown you many great miracles from the Father. For which of these do you stone me?" (John 10:32).

"The Pharisee stood up and prayed about himself" (Luke 18:11).

"It is not right to take the children's bread and toss it to their dogs" (Mark 7:27).

"If I drive out demons by Beelzebub, by whom do your followers drive them out?" (Luke 11:19).

"Do not announce it [almsgiving] with trumpets" (Matthew 6:2).
"You are like whitewashed tombs" (Matthew 23:27).
"You build tombs for the prophets and decorate the graves of the righteous" (Matthew 23:29).

What are some other striking passages you would add to this list? Name as many of the figures of speech as you can.

Not to confine your attention to isolated passages, read the discourse of Jesus on "the end of the world" in Matthew 24 and 25, noting the wonderful imagery.

Imagery is the poetic element in prose. It adds a bright and sparkling quality. This effect is due to emotion combined with imagination. It increases the pleasure of both listening and reading.

Great teachers, especially teachers of ultimate things, must have a poetic cast of mind, to suggest to learners more than can be told about truth. Such a teacher's mind can play with truth; it is not in bondage to literal facts. Could you name half a dozen such world teachers?

But imagery easily leads to misunderstanding, if it is read as prose by prosaic minds. Jesus was not only a master of imagery; he also sensed the danger of its being misunderstood and warned against it: "The words I have spoken to you are spirit and they are life" (John 6:63). "The letter kills, but the Spirit gives life" (2 Corinthians 3:6). Imagery means not what it says but what it means to say. The observance of this principle of exegesis would prevent many a dispute.

The New Testament rewritten without imagery would be less subject to misunderstanding, but it would be stale and flat, even if such a rewriting were possible. Try to state the meaning without imagery of "You are the salt of the earth. . . . You are the light of the world." Such an effort reveals how Jesus saved words, packed words with meaning, feathered them with imagery, and set them flying on the winds of the world. He taught with emphatic seriousness: "But I tell you that men will have to give account on the day of judgment for every careless word they have spoken" (Matthew 12:36).

What does a study of the imagery of Jesus mean for us practically? What effect has it on our reading of the New Testament? If we could use word pictures, how would it affect our teaching?

14

MEETING CROWDS

Did Jesus as a moral and religious teacher make his appeals primarily to crowds or to individuals?

What is your first impression? Think it over carefully and note whether your first impression is confirmed.

Which is the customary view, that Jesus worked mainly with crowds or with individuals?

Is the question itself valuable enough to consider? It has some bearing on the method of any Christian worker: Should he endeavor to reach crowds or individuals?

Does a great evangelist appeal primarily to crowds or to individuals? Was the work of Jesus of this type?

Should today's program of the church follow the method of Jesus?

Give some answer, however tentative, to these questions now. Our study may change some of your answers.

What are some of the crowd occasions in the life of Jesus?

Repeatedly he taught in the synagogues on the Sabbath day, especially in Galilee, including Capernaum and Nazareth. Many of his cures were wrought on these occasions, some of which we will note presently.

Is it not significant that when his home city rejected him, he should choose as a center of operations a larger and more centrally located city, Capernaum? "Then he went down to Capernaum, a town in Galilee, and on the Sabbath began to teach the people" (Luke 4:31; compare Matthew 4:13–17).

During the second year of his public ministry, "the year of popularity," he was constantly accompanied by crowds, from Capernaum, from other parts of Galilee, from Decapolis (the ten towns), from Jerusalem and Judea, from beyond Jordan, from Idumea in the extreme south, and from Tyre and Sidon in the west. Just how large these multitudes were we cannot say, but the feeding of the four thousand and the five thousand, besides women and children, may give us some idea. There was a period when the new teacher gave every appearance of being backed by a popular movement. These crowds, it is true, for the most part did not really understand that his call involved sacrifice. They came to be healed, to see works of healing, to see the new rabbi, to hear his wonderful words, and even to eat of the loaves and fishes. Rumors and reports helped to bring them.

Jesus seems to have directed his work mainly toward the cities and villages (Luke 8:1-3). "I must go also into the next towns," he would say. He worked by design in the centers of population, though not exclusively there. He would send messengers ahead to prepare the village for his coming. He saw cities, as he saw multitudes, as he saw women, as he saw children, as, too, he saw individuals. Some of these cities later he rebuked because they did not repent, though mighty works had been done in them: Bethsaida, Korazin, and Capernaum.

At times Jesus suffered inconvenience because of the crowds. They thronged him, they kept him so busy that at times he and the disciples had not enough leisure to eat, they kept his mother and his brothers from getting to him, they followed him when he would try to leave them behind, they awaited his coming on the other side of the lake, they continued with him for days, they would even come to take him by force to make him king.

Was Jesus the master as well as the ministering servant of crowds? He had compassion on them as sheep scattered without a shepherd. He would have them sit down by companies and would feed them. He would send them away, after first telling his disciples where to go. By what method did he bid them depart? He would leave them and go up to the mountain to pray, or take his disciples away into a desert place to rest. He would get into a boat and speak to them as they gathered on the lakeside. He would heal their sick, as many as came. He would teach them the Beatitudes and other wonderful words of life.

A multitude was present when he healed the paralytic in the synagogue in Capernaum, and the man with the withered hand, and the servant of the centurion, and the dumb demoniac. Can you find other instances of healing when a multitude was present?

A great multitude went with him to Nain when the widow's son was raised, and to the home of Jairus when his daughter was raised, and to the home of Martha and Mary when Lazarus was raised.

Jesus attended the annual religious festivals (Passover, Dedication, Tabernacles) of the Jews in Jerusalem where there were always crowds. Once he cleansed the temple at such a time, as well as taught and healed.

He freely attended festive social gatherings, like the wedding at Cana, or the great feast made for him in Capernaum by Matthew Levi, one of his chosen disciples, or the dinner in the home of Simon the Pharisee in Bethany. And something always happened when he was guest. Or was it the case that no record was made of the social occasions he graced when nothing happened? Can you find other such occasions of a social nature?

To the multitude he praised the faith of the Roman centurion, eulogized John the Baptist, spoke parables as a mode of selection from the crowd, gave the Sermon on the Mount, told them to believe on him whom God had sent, spoke of "the bread of life," justified healing on the Sabbath, extended the invitation at the Feast of Tabernacles to come to him and drink, and warned them against the leaven of the Pharisees. What else did he say upon different occasions to the multitudes? Note particularly Luke 14:25–35.

In what esteem did the multitudes hold Jesus? It was very different at different times. They were amazed at his works, they heard his words gladly because of the note of authority, they held that a great prophet had arisen among them, that God had visited his people, that he had done all things well, that it was never so seen in Israel, that the Messiah himself could not do more wonderful signs, that he was John the Baptist, or Elijah, or Jeremiah, or one of the old prophets, or the son of David, that he was a Samaritan and had a devil, that he was beside himself, that he should be crucified.

Can you find still other expressions of the popular mind concerning him?

What do you think about Jesus' preference concerning crowds or individuals?

Let us see some of the individuals to whom he ministered. Recall as many as you can. They include each of the Twelve, Nicodemus, the woman of Samaria, the son of the nobleman at Capernaum, the man with the spirit of an unclean devil, Peter's wife's mother, the leper, the paralytic, the thirty-eight-year-old invalid at Bethesda's pool, the man with the withered hand, the servant of the centurion in Capernaum, the son of the

widow of Nain, the woman who anointed him, Simon the Pharisee, Mary
Magdalene, Joanna, Susanna, the dumb demoniac, the woman of the
multitude who blessed the womb that bore him, the two Gadarene
demoniacs, the daughter of Jairus, the two blind men, the daughter of
the Syrophoenician, the deaf stammerer, the blind man of Bethsaida, the
demoniac boy, the woman taken in adultery, the seventy sent on a mission two by two, the questioning lawyers (two), the Pharisee who invited
him to dinner, one of the lawyers who felt that Jesus cast a reproach on
his friends, one of the multitude who wanted Jesus to divide an inheritance for him, the woman who could not stand straight, Herod, the man
with the dropsy, the ten lepers, the rich young ruler, Martha, Mary, Lazarus,
one born blind, the mother of James and John, the two blind men at
Jericho, one of whom was Bartimaeus, Zacchaeus, Caiaphas, Pilate, the
thief on the cross, and his mother.

Are some omitted? How many are here?

What had Jesus done for these individuals?

How many of these individuals had Jesus served in the presence of a
crowd? How many privately?

Why did he sometimes take the afflicted individual out of the city or
crowd in order to effect a cure?

Was any group cure effected? (Would that of the ten lepers be such?)

Is it fair to say that in some way personal relations had been established with each of the seventy who were sent out two by two?

What shall we now say as to whether Jesus dealt by preference with
crowds or individuals?

Can we be sure of our answer?

Does the Great Commission put emphasis on the crowd or on the
individual?

Which was more lasting, his work with crowds or that with individuals?

Does the resurrected Christ today still minister to crowds or only to
individual disciples?

In the teaching concerning the speck and beam in the eye, some think
Jesus underestimated the value of public judgment and social criticism.
What do you think?

Doubtless for some persons it is better to work with crowds, for others
it is better to work with individuals.

With whom was his most careful work done, crowds or individuals, if
we can distinguish degrees of carefulness in his work?

It is true that often he reached crowds by means of individuals, when any act of healing or word of teaching was done for an individual in the presence of a crowd.

And it is also true that often he reached individuals by means of the crowds to whom he spoke. Some who came to scoff remained to pray. Others who came to take him went away charmed by his matchless words.

A personal conclusion: Jesus began with individuals, continued with crowds, and ended with individuals, during the three successive main periods of his ministry. He worked by preference and most successfully with individuals, because of the very nature of crowds. In fact, he did not trust crowds.

15

MODELING

W hat does this title suggest to you?

It is a pedagogical truism that we teach more by what we are than by what we say. Such is the influence of personality. We learn by association with persons. All that goes by the name of suggestion and imitation is at work when one person is placed in contact with another.

The great moral and religious teachers of all time have associated with themselves a group of intimate learners, or disciples, that they might learn not so much the lessons as the way of their teacher, so that, by personal witness, the truth might be passed on to others and through them to others. So did Confucius, so did Buddha, so did John the Baptist, and so did Jesus. Some of his disciples in turn likewise had associates, as Mark with Peter. Paul, too, had associates in his work, Silas, Barnabas, and others (see Acts 13:1-3).

Jesus attached these learners to himself by calling them, once, twice, or even perhaps three times, under different circumstances. Andrew and John had first been disciples of the Baptist, who directed their attention to Jesus. Then they were called once or twice by the lakeside. The words of the call were few, simple, direct, personal: "Follow me." In the first intent it was a call to personal association and then to all that might flow from it.

Mark 3:14 makes it plain that the purpose of the call was that they might first be "with him" and then that he might "send them." Thus the main secret of the training of the Twelve was association and its main objective was service.

These twelve chosen ones, perhaps twelve because of the tribes of Israel, were Galilean fishermen, and tax gatherers, and others. Only Judas was from Judea. They were all innocent of the learning of the rabbinical schools of their time. Their occupations show this, but they were not ignorant of the religious customs of the Jews, which were theirs also. Doubtless Jesus regarded them as fresh wineskins, fit receptacles of his own new wine of religious truth. They were not always apt pupils, but their hearts were loyal, except that of Judas at the end, and though the Crucifixion was a rude jolt to all their hopes, the Resurrection restored their confidence. So in the end that which they had seen and heard through personal association, "the grace and truth that came through Jesus Christ," was triumphant in their lives. Someone has defined Christianity as "the contagion of a divine personality."

There seem to have been several concentric circles of persons about Jesus. In the innermost circle came Peter, James, and John, of whom John seems to have been nearest the heart of Jesus. Then came the others of the Twelve. Then perhaps the seventy disciples. Then perhaps the company of the ministering women (Luke 8:2-3). Then the multitudes. Finally the hostile critics. The line of division was the degree of spiritual insight. To each and all Jesus gave himself according to their receptive ability. To all, the parables were spoken, to the chosen few the mysteries were explained.

Would you say that Jesus individualized his learners? Think carefully of this question. Some of the disciples of Jesus appear to us now as vague personalities. What do we know of Bartholomew, and James the son of Alphaeus? What finally became of the seventy who had been sent out?

Some students of the temperaments of the early followers of Jesus have concluded that Peter was nervous, John was sanguine, Philip was phlegmatic, and that each of the disciples not only had a distinct temperament but also was chosen on this account by Jesus, who in doing so revealed his power to influence all types of people. How do these views impress you? Some regard Paul as choleric.

To make our study of the individualizing of the disciples by Jesus concrete, let us consider the most obvious case, that of his treatment of Peter.

Recall the characteristics of Peter and the way of training him used by Jesus.

The records represent Peter as having "the precipitate will," that is, he was impulsive, rash, impetuous, bold. Perhaps his opposite in all these respects was Thomas. Peter's name usually heads the list of the disciples, though he was not the first called. His leadership seemed natural. He was the regular spokesman for the group, not that he had been so delegated. It was Peter who answered for all the decisive question: "Who do you say I am?" On the Mount of Transfiguration he wanted to build material tabernacles for spiritual beings. He alone would prove that the appearance on the water was Jesus, by walking out to him. He it was who began to rebuke Jesus for proposing to submit to suffering. He alone of the disciples protested against his feet being washed by Jesus. Most stoutly of all he affirmed he would not deny Jesus. He rashly drew his sword and needlessly cut off the ear of the servant of the high priest. Though John outran him to the tomb, Peter was the first to enter. He cast aside his garment and swam ashore to meet his recognized and resurrected Lord. These are some of the things that show the kind of man Peter was.

How did Jesus develop Peter?

He called him to a difficult task, to catch men alive. Such tasks help to tame impetuous natures.

He gave him a new name: in the Hebrew it is Cephas, in the Greek Peter, signifying what he wanted him to become.

He visited him in his Capernaum home and healed a sick member of his family.

He placed heavy responsibility upon him, giving him "the keys," making him the group leader.

He allowed him to do an adventurous thing and fail, trying to walk on water. Not that Peter, being a fisherman and a swimmer, should have felt fear at beginning to sink.

He rebuked him: "Get behind me, Satan," a rather humiliating address to one who had just been made the keeper of the keys.

He corrected his reliance on physical force: "Put your sword away."

He warned him concerning the denial: "Before the rooster crows, you will disown me three times." Was this really a warning or a statement of a predestined fact?

After the denial, Jesus forgave Peter and recommissioned him. The resurrection angel mentioned Peter especially by name: "Go tell his disciples, and Peter." The repeated commission given Peter: "Feed my lambs," "take care of my sheep," "feed my sheep," bound Peter again in personal loyalty to his Lord.

Did this training make Peter rocklike? Tradition says that on suffering crucifixion under persecution, Peter requested that it might be with head down, that he die not as his Lord.

Can you similarly suggest the characters of James and John, and how Jesus trained them? Did John begin by being an apostle of love, as he ended?

Can you mention some of the features of the group training that the Twelve received? For example, in caring for the physical body? in encouragement? in prayer? in love? Consult Mark 6:31; 5:36; Luke 22:32; John 13:1.

What is the significance of the fact that Jesus would address the disciples at times as "children" or "little flock"? See Mark 2:5; 10:24; Luke 12:32; John 13:33; 21:5.

What are some differences between a teacher today before his class and Jesus with the Twelve?

The Twelve were dependent on Jesus for their training. Was he also in a measure dependent on them for companionship and strength? See Luke 22:28, and remember the agony in the garden.

Name some respects in which Christianity in its history has exemplified this same reliance on the principle of human association.

What further additions would you make to this discussion?

16

PSYCHOLOGICAL FACTORS

Did Jesus stimulate the instincts and innate reactions of people? If so, he touched the original springs of all action, he sounded the depths of human nature. If not, his appeal does not reach down to the oldest elements in the human frame.

The question is important, for it helps us to understand whether Jesus released all the energies of human nature, and in what sense, and so we may see whether and to what extent his teachings meet the profoundest needs and demands of human nature.

What are these innate reactions? They include fear; curiosity; pugnacity; pride; love; sex; gregariousness; ownership; sympathy; imitation; play; rivalry; habit; temperament.

Whether Jesus himself evinced all the instincts of man we cannot now consider, nor can we exhaustively deal with the main question and show from the Gospels all the appeals to each of the innate reactions of people.

At this point, go carefully through the list and check those to which upon reflection you think Jesus did appeal. Are there any omissions? If so, which? Are you fairly sure about the entries checked? It is a new question, this reading of the teachings of Jesus in terms of biology, and one probably very far from his own consciousness, but it is one in which people today are very interested. Let us examine the above list.

Fear. This was not the primary appeal of Jesus. And he never appealed to slavish fear, as perhaps Jonathan Edwards did in his sermon on "Sinners in the Hands of an Angry God." Yet Jesus did appeal to fear in the sense of reverential awe, perhaps in the same sense in which Solomon had taught: "The fear of the LORD is the beginning of wisdom." Thus

Jesus says, "Do not be afraid of those who kill the body and after that can do no more. But I will show you whom you should fear: Fear him who, after the killing of the body, has power to throw you into hell. Yes, I tell you, fear him. [Does this refer to God or the Devil? Read on.] Are not five sparrows sold for two pennies? Yet not one of them is forgotten by God. Indeed, the very hairs of your head are all numbered. Don't be afraid; you are worth more than many sparrows" (Luke 12:4-7).

This teaching was given to his friends, not to the crowds. Likewise to his disciples he said, "Do not let not your hearts be troubled and do not be afraid" (John 14:27).

Yet his teaching constantly made reference to the house built on the sands whose fall was great, to weeping and wailing and gnashing of teeth, to the undying worm and the unquenched fire, to the outer darkness, to the broad way leading to destruction and to the many going that way, and to those who at the judgment would call on the rocks and hills to fall on them, and to the wicked who, separated from the righteous, should go away into the punishment of the ages.

We conclude then that while the motive of fear is not the biggest thing in the appeal of Jesus (what is?), yet he did use the innate fear reaction. Running away and hiding, which he associates with the Last Judgment, are expressions of fear. When do Christians make the motive of fear the main appeal?

Curiosity. The figure of Jesus was constantly the center of curiosity, wonder, amazement, and astonishment, caused now by his physical presence, as when going up to Jerusalem for the last time; now by some teaching, as by the Sermon on the Mount; and now by some work of healing. But we cannot say Jesus ever worked a miracle in order to amaze people. That would have been like casting himself down from the pinnacle of the temple, which he regarded as a temptation from the Evil One. One of the reputed sayings of Jesus exactly covers the point: "Wonder at what you see!" Zacchaeus was curious to see Jesus. Herod was curious to see some miracle at his hands. The emotion of wonder clearly enters into the beholding of the lilies of the field, clothed of God. What we wonder at we tend to approach and examine. So the response of Jesus to the inquiry of the two disciples of John as to his abode, "Come, . . . and you will see," is not only companionable but also attractive to the instinct of curiosity. The promise of Jesus to Nathanael, "You shall see heaven open, and the angels of God ascending and descending on the Son of Man," must have awakened a wondering interest. Have you still other illustrations?

Pugnacity. Much debate has raged around the Christian appeal to this instinct. The fighting instinct may, however, be directed toward overcoming social evils by methods other than war. Paul catches the idea exactly when he urges, "Fight the good fight of faith." Jesus probably never appealed directly to the impulse to go to war ("My kingdom is not of this world. If it were, my servants would fight to prevent my arrest by the Jews," John 18:36), though some of his teachings may consistently involve going to war ("Give to Caesar what is Caesar's," one of which was military service, Mark 12:17). Jesus felt that he came to destroy the works of the Devil. This warfare he conducted and commissioned his disciples to conduct. He himself was angered, which is the fighting feeling, when his critics objected to his healing on the Sabbath day. So the characteristic thing that Jesus did to the fighting instinct was to sublimate it, to give it a moral equivalent, to redirect it. He was so far from allowing murderous killing that he condemned its cause, saying, "But I tell you that anyone who is angry with his brother will be subject to judgment" (Matthew 5:22). What else would you say about the appeal of Jesus to pugnacity?

Pride. This instinct is the basis of all self-display. It presupposes spectators, those whose admiration one seeks. Jesus recognized it in others but he did not exemplify it in himself. There is nothing to indicate that he appealed to it in others. Or do you dissent from this view? Of course the name of the instinct must not mislead us; we must look at its meaning. Jesus often asserted himself in expressing unpopular views, but upon such self-assertion he did not express pride. Had you thought we should find direct appeals to all our innate reactions in the teachings of Jesus? There are phases of human nature to which he makes no appeal. Can you now anticipate others?

Love. Here we reach the main appeal of Jesus. It was to the hearts of men. Jesus himself had the parental instinct keenly developed, due possibly in measure to his guardianship over his younger siblings in his home in Nazareth. His was the tender emotion—he was moved by compassion at any distress, he put his arms about children, he protected even the guilty. He could go no further in his appeal than when he included even enemies in the scope of love. It was to him, as to others, the great commandment in the law. The law had enjoined equality of love between self and neighbor. Jesus extended the commandment in its new form to the point of sacrifice of physical life, "as I have loved you." This is both the novelty and the core of his teaching. Why, then, does he say one must "hate his father and his mother"?

Sex. Is there any appeal in the teachings of Jesus to the sex instinct? He recognized it, did not forbid marriage, taught purity of thought as a preventive measure against adulterous acts, and allowed that for the sake of the kingdom of heaven some might refrain completely from sex. But there is no direct or indirect appeal of Jesus to the sex nature of man.

Gregariousness. The company of the disciples with Jesus as their leader, sending some out two by two, the founding of the church, the rejection of the ascetic life of John the Baptist—all show the recognition of and appeal to this instinct.

Ownership. One of the fundamental objections to any form of dictatorship, in contrast to democratic institutions, is that it runs counter to the human instinct of acquisition, on which the right of private ownership rests. Did Jesus appeal to this instinct? No, not directly, but he sublimated it; that is, he redirected it to spiritual instead of material ends. He urged that treasures be laid up not on earth but in heaven. The trouble with the rich fool in the parable was that he provided only material things for his soul. The trouble with the rich man, unlike Lazarus, was that he made no heavenly friends. The trouble with the rich young ruler was that his affection, possibly not realized by himself until his conversation with Jesus, had been set on things on the earth.

In all this teaching the acquisitive instinct is centered on things above, not on things on the earth. Yet Jesus did not negate the acquisitive instinct for material things; he only subordinated it. Thus he taught that when the interests of the kingdom had been placed first, all these things of earth, food, drink, and clothing, would be added (Matthew 6:33). Besides, he taught that all forms of sacrifice were returned a hundred times even in this present world. "I tell you the truth . . . no one who has left home or brothers or sisters or mother or father or children or fields for me and the gospel will fail to receive a hundred times as much in this present age (homes, brothers, sisters, mothers, children and fields—and with them, persecutions) and in the age to come, eternal life" (Mark 10:29-30; see also Luke 18:28-29).

In what sense is this true?

We conclude, then, that Jesus did appeal to the acquisitive instinct for material things but only in an indirect and subordinate way, while directing it mainly to the attainment of spiritual things.

Would you modify this conclusion?

Sympathy. The sharing of feeling is natural. We become affected by the feelings of others, and they are affected by ours. This applies to feelings not only of sorrow but also of joy, fear, anger, curiosity. Sympathy thus is social. It covers so many emotional states and is induced in us by so many different emotions in others that it is better to regard it as a general, or nonspecific, innate tendency, rather than an instinct.

Did Jesus appeal to this tendency? Inevitably. Jesus shared the emotions of others, as at the gate of Nain, the tomb of Lazarus, and in the home of Jairus. He recognized and commended sympathy in the parable of the Good Samaritan. He taught that the companions of the bridegroom should not fast and be sad in his presence. Can we imagine Jesus at the wedding feast of Cana being emotionally isolated from the festive company?

Can you recall other pertinent incidents from the Gospels?

To what extent do you suppose the disciples shared the anger of Jesus in the synagogue when the paralytic was healed? or his righteous indignation at the cleansing of the temple? or his amazement in the garden?

Imitation. We sympathize with feelings, we suggest ideas, we imitate acts. Invention marks Jesus rather than imitation. Yet he does imitate, and he does especially appeal to the instinct of imitation. He imitated John in having disciples; he imitated the prophets in speaking parables, though he improved upon their models; he followed custom in sitting to teach; and naturally he acquired the Aramaic speech in childhood by imitation, as well as the art of the carpenter. Note, imitation may be unintentional as well as intentional.

Do you hesitate to think of Jesus as under the influence of imitation? Why?

Jesus makes special appeal to the instinct of imitation in his disciples, sensing himself as their model. "Follow me"; "[let him] take up his cross"; "It is enough for the student to be like his teacher, and the servant like his master"; "Now that I, your Lord and Teacher, have washed your feet, you also should wash one another's feet"; "I have set you an example" (John 13:15). Note especially this instance: "Be perfect, therefore, as your heavenly Father is perfect" (Matthew 5:48), coming at the end of a description of the Father's impartiality.

What other illustrations have you in mind?

Play. The role of play in modern education and life is so large and so valuable that we should like to find that Jesus appealed to the impulse of play in man. But the evidence is remote and indirect. Jesus must have played as a boy, for (1) no boy who does not play can have the social development that Jesus later exemplified; (2) as a man he attracted children, which no man without play in his nature can do; (3) he recalled the play of children in his comments on people (Matthew 11:17); and (4) he contrasted himself with the ascetic John. This evidence is not conclusive, but it is strongly circumstantial.

Can you add other items? Or would you subtract from these?

Rivalry. Jesus did not think of himself as the rival of any but modestly named himself "the Son of Man," the appellation by which the Spirit was accustomed to speak to Ezekiel. To avoid any clash or competition in baptizing with the disciples of John, Jesus withdrew from Judea into Galilee (John 4:1-3). He checked ambitious rivalry in the group of the disciples, teaching that the greatest is the servant of all. In the kingdom there are appeals to do one's duty and rewards for doing it, but there is no appeal to outstrip another. Jesus disclaimed the power to assign right and left hand seats: "To sit at my right or left is not for me to grant. These places belong to those for whom they have been prepared" (Mark 10:40). Lower seats are to be taken until one is bidden to come up higher. One is to strive to enter in at the straight gate but not to get in ahead of another. Paul uses the appeal to ambition three or more times, for example, "make it your ambition to lead a quiet life" (1 Thessalonians 4:11), but not once does this word appear in the Gospels.

Habit. The tendency to repeat an act once done is characteristic of all living tissue. No teacher could fail to utilize it. Jesus acquired habits, as for example attendance at the synagogue service on the Sabbath. And certain of the virtues he extolled presuppose the formation of habit, for example, putting one's hand to the plow and not looking back. Can you illustrate further?

Temperament. No two people have exactly the same temperament, because the physical make-up of each is different. Temperament is the effect of these constitutional conditions on our mental life, especially on its affective tone. It is to some extent alterable by such influences as climate, food, and disease. Jesus had temperament, and so did each of the disciples, and so did all others mentioned in the Gospels. But all attempts at classifying temperaments are baffled by the complexity of the facts, though we still speak of a phlegmatic temperament and other kinds. Though we think of Peter as impetuous, James and John as ambitious "sons of thunder," Thomas as doubting, Andrew as practical, Judas as earthbound, Nathanael as meditative, and others in still other ways, we hardly know their temperaments well enough to say whether Jesus appealed to them or not. In a general way we do know that he successfully related to eleven of them, that Peter became rocklike, and John an apostle of love, and that persons of diverse temperaments are found among Christians today. In general, we conclude that the evidence is lacking to answer the question whether Jesus utilized the temperaments of people in his appeals.

Or would you say differently?

Reviewing, is there more in this matter of the appeal of Jesus to the innate reactions of man than you had supposed?

What significance have these facts for you?

How close to the bedrock of human nature do they show Jesus to have been? Yet, how far removed from original human nature in his goal?

No one would think of claiming that Jesus consciously made all these appeals to the specific and general tendencies of men. The only claim is that his teaching, when analyzed, contains these appeals.

17

LEARNING BY DOING

No reception without reaction, no impression without correlative expression is a great maxim that the teacher ought never to forget. Learning by doing is basic to most learning.

Did Jesus use the method of impression? How?

Did he also use the method of expression? How?

Prepare two parallel lists of examples of his use of impression and expression.

On which method, impression or expression, do you think he placed the greater emphasis?

Did Jesus rather tell people what to think or stimulate them to think?

Was it his aim to get a system of thought accepted or to develop a certain type of conduct?

Did he care more for the creed or the deed?

People think differently about the answers to these questions, and it is your privilege to have your own opinion based on the gospel records.

Looking through the chapters of this book we may agree that some of the methods of Jesus relate to receiving while others deal with doing.

Is impression the means and expression the end? Or is expression the means and impression the end?

Where did Jesus place the primary emphasis, on receiving or doing?

There is another way of approaching the study of these two methods. Make a list of some things that Jesus gave his students to do. What actions did he secure from them?

Compare your list with the following.

"Come."
"Follow."

"Go."
"Sell."
"Preach."
"Watch."
"Pray."
"Do likewise."
"Wash."
"Offer the gift."
"Stretch out your hand."
"Take away the stone."
"Come down."
"Go and tell."
"Sin no more."
"Feed my sheep."
"Make disciples of all nations."
"Find a donkey."
"Give to Caesar."
"Show yourself to the priest."
"Get up, take your mat."
"Give them something to eat."
"Work."
"Make them come in."
"Turn to him the other [cheek]."

Do you get the impression that Jesus made his pupils inactive or active? What happens to a learner's ideas when he does something?

There is a sense in which it is true that doing depends on thinking; there is also a sense in which it is true that thinking depends on doing. Can you figure out which of these two propositions is true? And the sense in which both are true?

It is true that all our voluntary action depends on thinking. It is also true that all our clear and accurate thinking depends on having had experience in the field in which we think. Relatively little of our action is based on thinking, though this little is of critical importance. The most of our action is due to instinct, impulse, imitation, suggestion, and habit. Without doubt, when Jesus made people think, they often acted better; also when he made them act, they thought.

Do you get the impression that he rather approached action by way of thought, or thought by way of action?

If we make action a function of thought, we are idealists; if we make thought a function of action, we are pragmatists. To the idealist, thinking is primary and action secondary; to the pragmatist, action is primary and thought secondary.

Was Jesus an idealist or a pragmatist?

What are some of the things that Jesus gave men to think about? Make a list of them. Compare your list with the following.

God is Father.
Men are brothers.
The kingdom of heaven is spiritual.
The kingdom of heaven is social and at hand.
Jesus is the Messiah of the Jews.
Jesus is God's Son.
Jesus is man's son.
The soul lives after death.
Sin is due to ignorance or willfulness.

Does this list change your view as to whether Jesus placed primary emphasis on the idea or the act? Acts secured are expression, ideas communicated are impression.

There is still another interesting mode of approach to the study of Jesus' primary appeal. Jesus gave men things to do; he also gave them ideas to hold. Did he also give them things to feel? What emotional attitudes did Jesus awaken in men? Make a list of such emotions. Is Jesus more of a mystic than an idealist or a pragmatist?

Some feelings awakened in people by Jesus:

Awe
Reverence
Thanksgiving
Dependence
Trust
Faith
Hope
Love
Righteous indignation
Peace
Sympathy
Joy

Would you add to this list? Of course, some of these emotions are complex and involve attitudes of will as well as ideas.

Is the primary call of Jesus then to action? or to think? or to feel? Feeling is an effect of both ideas and acts; it may result from impression or expression; it may also inspire both thinking and acting.

Did people always do what Jesus told them to do? Remember the rich young ruler. When they did do so, why did they? That is, how did Jesus secure action? This is something we should all like to know. People usually did as Jesus said because

He did not request, he commanded with authority.

He inspired self-confidence and confidence in himself.

His magnetic personality awoke responses.

He was obviously doing big things and knew what he was about.

He had both moral and physical force.

His healings awakened gratitude.

He divided the good from the bad and appealed to the hope of reward and the fear of punishment.

Would you add to these?

In what ways may this study help us in our work?

Would you rather give a person an idea, awaken a feeling, or set a task? Which one of these three is most effective?

The following conclusion may not be correct: Jesus cared more for expression than impression. He used impression as a means to expression. He cared more for what men did than for what they thought or how they felt. He himself was more of a pragmatist than an idealist or a mystic. To him ideas were functions of acts rather than acts being functions of ideas.

Some quotations:

"If anyone chooses to do God's will, he will find out whether my teaching comes from God or whether I speak on my own" (John 7:17).

"Thus, by their fruit you will recognize them" (Matthew 7:20).

"Now that you know these things, you will be blessed if you do them" (John 13:17).

"Not every one who says to me, 'Lord, Lord,' . . . but only he who does the will of my Father who is in heaven" (Matthew 7:21).

"Therefore everyone who hears these words of mine and puts them into practice is like a wise man who built his house on the rock" (Matthew 7:24).

"Whatever you did for one of the least of these brothers of mine, you did for me" (Matthew 25:40).

"But whoever lives by the truth comes into the light" (John 3:21).

18

ATTITUDE TOWARD CHILDREN

Why should God come into human life in the form of an infant?

Why should this infant pass through all the stages of human growth right up to maturity?

What biblical word, if any, reveals more of God's goodness and love than the word *child*?

Do the birth stories of Matthew and Luke glorify only the infancy of Jesus or all childhood?

So Jesus experienced all the processes and stages of development.

When he became a man, how would you characterize his attitude toward children?

How did this attitude differ from that of the disciples? See Matthew 19:13.

Which one of these two attitudes was more characteristic of the times?

What motives led people to bring their children to Jesus? See Luke 18:15.

What emancipating words for childhood did Jesus speak? See Mark 10:14.

How was he affected by the interference of the disciples? See Mark 10:14. (Have you noticed that Mark, though the briefest gospel, has the fullest references to the emotions of Jesus?)

Make a list of all the things that Jesus did for children. Support each item by a reported instance or by clear deduction from such. How long is your list? Compare it with the following.

Some things Jesus did for children:

1. He took them in his arms and blessed them.
2. He provided for their physical wants in feeding the four and five thousand, "besides women and children." He commanded that some food be given to the daughter of Jairus (Mark 5:43).
3. He healed them. How many were boys? See John 4:46–54 and Matthew 17:14–21. How many were girls? See Mark 7:24–30 and Matthew 9:18–26. Are there still others? May he have healed some not recorded? See Mark 1:32–34.
4. He observed the manner of their play and life. He noted their game of wedding and funeral (Luke 7:32), their sleeping in bed with their father (Luke 11:7), and the good gifts they had received from their parents (Matthew 7:11). What other things had he observed?

With what emotions did Jesus regard children? Write down all you can, with your reasons in each case. Compare your answers with the following list.

How Jesus felt about children:

1. He felt indignant that his own disciples should stand between the children and him, and so revealed his interest in their welfare.
2. He used the diminutive of affection combined with an endearing term in raising the daughter of Jairus, saying, *Talitha koum* (Mark 5:41), "Lambkin, arise." From all he did for them we conclude that he loved them. Compare the tender words to Peter: "Feed my lambs" (John 21:15; also Mark 7:27).
3. He must have regarded them with a kind of sacred awe, "for I tell you that their angels in heaven always see the face of my Father in heaven" (Matthew 18:10). What does this saying mean?
4. He felt respect for them, for he taught us not to despise them. See Matthew 18:10.
5. He felt sympathy for them. To the women of Jerusalem bewailing his fate, he said, "Weep for yourselves and for your children" (Luke 23:28).

So some of the emotions with which Jesus regarded children are interest in their welfare, love, awe, respect, and sympathy.
Have you other emotions to report?
Have you additional illustrations of these?

What are some of the ideas that Jesus had about children? Give quotations or references to support your views. Some of these ideas have already been suggested.

Compare your views with the following ideas that Jesus had about children:

1. They are a type of true greatness and of membership in the kingdom. "Therefore, whoever humbles himself like this child is the greatest in the kingdom of heaven" (Matthew 18:4). "The kingdom of heaven belongs to such as these" (Matthew 19:14).
2. They are not to be offended. "And if anyone causes one of these little ones who believe in me to sin, it would be better for him to be thrown into the sea with a large millstone tied around his neck" (Mark 9:42). Could this refer to those young in the faith, as well as to children?
3. They are identified by him with himself. "Whoever welcomes one of these little children in my name welcomes me" (Mark 9:37). Is this saying commonly realized?
4. They are specific objects of the Father's loving purpose. "In the same way your Father in heaven is not willing that any of these little ones should be lost" (Matthew 18:14).

In what higher esteem could children be held? They typify the heavenly kingdom in humility, trust, and service; they are not to be despised or caused to stumble; receiving them is receiving Christ, and receiving Christ is receiving God; their guardian angels do not have to wait for the Father's favor but always see his face; they themselves are individual objects of his providential will.

Did children come to Jesus readily? Were they happy in his company? What does this show as to the element of childhood in his own nature? Did they ever sing his praises? See Matthew 21:15. What was their song?

Jesus said in prayer: "I praise you, Father, Lord of heaven and earth, because you have hidden these things from the wise and learned, and revealed them to little children" (Matthew 11:25).

Also he quoted the Psalms in defense of the children singing his praises: "From the lips of children and infants you have ordained praise" (Matthew 21:16).

Are these views true?

What difference would they make in our practice if we acted upon them?

Jesus sometimes addressed his adult disciples as children. Have you some illustrations of this? What is their significance? See John 13:33; 21:5.

In what respects do we commonly fail to exemplify love, truth, and freedom in our attitude toward children?

What modifications in our behavior as parents and teachers would you propose in the light of Jesus' attitude toward children?

If all childhood is divine, "for of such is the kingdom of heaven" (KJV), what kind of adulthood, if any, is no less so?

19

CHARACTERISTICS OF GOOD TEACHERS

In one way it is fruitless to enumerate the personal qualifications for teaching, because they are so many and so general.

We may use the qualities of Jesus as a teacher, his characteristics as the great teacher, as a concrete ideal standard by which to measure ourselves.

What other advantages might follow from such a study?

Formulate first in your own mind the characteristics that any world-class teacher should possess.

In the following list check off the ones you regard as essential.

The essential qualifications of a world-class teacher:

1. A vision that encompasses the world
2. Knowledge of the nature of humanity
3. Mastery of the subject taught
4. Aptness in teaching
5. A life that models the teaching

Do you regard each of these as necessary for a world-class teacher?

Would you add to this list of minimum essentials?

Now consider whether Jesus had each of these qualifications.

1. Did his vision encompass the world?

"I have other sheep who are not of this sheep pen. I must bring them also." "But I, when I am lifted up from the earth, will draw all men to myself." "It [the kingdom of heaven] is like yeast that a woman took and mixed into a large amount of flour until it worked all through the dough." "Go into all the world and preach the good news to all creation."

What do you conclude?

Have you still other quotations?

2. Did Jesus know what human nature was like?

"He did not need man's testimony about man, for he knew what was in a man." "Why are you trying to trap me." "He saw through their duplicity." "Why are you talking among yourselves?" "Here is a true Israelite, in whom there is nothing false." "The fact is, you have had five husbands, and the man you now have is not your husband." The Samaritan woman said, "Come, see a man who told me everything I ever did.'"

Have you other quotations?

What do you conclude?

How do you explain the knowledge Jesus had of human nature in general and of particular individuals?

3. Again, was Jesus a master of the subject he taught? What was his subject? Was it science? or comparative literature, or morality and religion?

"No one ever spoke the way this man does." "He taught as one who had authority, and not as their teachers of the law." "How did this man get such learning?" "No one could say a word in reply, and from that day on no one dared to ask him any more questions."

Jesus revealed our spiritual nature and capacities in a way we hardly understand, and certainly cannot imitate.

4. Was Jesus a good teacher?

Think of those "unschooled, ordinary men" (Acts 4:13) whom Jesus chose to be his students, and what forceful personalities they became under his tutelage. Recall how the common people heard him gladly. Note his influence on Nicodemus, one of the rulers of the Jews. Remember that he never wrote, yet his words were not forgotten. Think of the books that have been written about his methods as a teacher. Have you other facts to cite?

From whom have we ourselves learned so much?

5. Did the life of Jesus embody his teaching?

"About all that Jesus began to do and to teach." "I am the way and the truth and the life." "If any one chooses to do God's will, he will find out whether my teaching comes from God or whether I speak on my own." "But whoever lives by the truth comes into the light." "Can any of you prove me guilty of sin?" "Now the prince of this world will be driven out." "This man has done nothing wrong." "I find no basis for a charge against him." "Surely he was the Son of God!" "I am gentle and humble in heart."

What is the effect of teaching that is not supported by living?

First Jesus did, and then he taught. His living was the dramatization of his teaching. The truth that he lived and taught was, in his own paradox, "Whoever loses his life for my sake will find it."

Shall we then conclude that Jesus fully possessed the five requisite qualifications of a world-class teacher? The fact that the centuries have shown him to be a world-class teacher would be proof for an affirmative answer. That his followers number more today than ever before and that they are full of faith and works, also show that in time all the world will know his teaching.

Once, with no thought of Jesus as teacher in mind, I listed the desirable qualities in a teacher. These were grouped under five headings, physical, intellectual, emotional, moral, and general. Then some time afterward it occurred to me to consider whether Jesus met these ideal specifications. With what result?

I will append the list and let you examine it.

Additional qualifications of the teacher:

I. Physical
1. Health
2. Good presence
3. A speaking eye
4. An effective voice
II. Intellectual
1. Common sense
2. Intelligence
3. Good language competence
4. Idealism
III. Emotional
1. Cheerfulness
2. Sympathy
3. Objectivity
4. Honor
5. Enthusiasm
6. Culture
7. Courtesy
IV. Volitional
1. Executive ability
2. Willingness to work

  3. Ambition
  4. Patience
  5. Humility
V. General
  1. A sense of vocation
  2. Sense of the greatness of the work
  3. Personality

How would you criticize this list for teachers?

Which of these characteristics does Jesus exemplify?

Did Jesus have ambition? Compare John 4:34; Luke 12:50. In what sense?

Is "personality" a comprehensive term that includes all the others?

How would you show that Jesus possessed the characteristics that you list for him? Do it for each one.

Would you change the grouping of any one of the characteristics?

Why is it desirable that teachers should have a sense of vocation? Did Jesus have one? Did Paul?

This standard was set up for the ideal teacher without Jesus being in mind. When applied to him, how does he meet the test? Shall we say, then, that he is an ideal teacher?

Of course, the list given above, made without thought of Jesus, does not do justice to him. What further characteristics, then, would you say he possessed?

A long list of characteristics could be made in answer to this question. Make your own list of significant additions to the one given above; check, in Figure 19.1, the characteristics you think Jesus possessed as teacher, and compare the two lists.

Justify each of the characteristics you have assigned him.

What contrasts do you find in his character?

What evidence of symmetry? Of serenity? What do you get out of an analytic study of this kind? Some students reject it as not worthwhile.

Some have suggested that artists should present Jesus as large, strong, beautiful, and personally magnetic.

Which of these four do you think he was?

The six essential qualities of the personality of the Christ are (1) life from within, (2) moral struggle, (3) complexity and compositeness, (4) exploration of all the higher powers of man, (5) being perennially in his prime, and (6) realization as far as possible of all ideals.

Physical strength	Love
Power to heal the body	Self-control
Skill	Self-sacrifice
Power over temptation	Self-respect
Loyalty	Sincerity
Courage	Joyousness
Prudence	Sorrow
Dignity	Intensity
Sinlessness	Anger
Social efficiency	Gratitude
Love of nature	Reverence
Love of children	Modesty
Pleasure in social life	Dependence
Friendliness	Prayerfulness
Passion for service	Artistic feeling
Reliance on others	Intuitive knowledge
Justice	Alertness
Authority	Positiveness
Love of truth	Dialectic skill
Information	Originality
Sense of mission	Spirituality

Figure 19.1. Some characteristics Jesus possessed as a teacher.

Of these six which ones does Jesus possess?

Another person has suggested that a teacher must first have an apti-
tude for vicariousness; second, an already accumulated wealth; third, an
ability to invigorate life through knowledge; fourth, a readiness to be
forgotten.

Which of these characteristics did Jesus possess? Was he ready to be
forgotten? Why?

Was Jesus scholarly? strict? teachable?

Check off your own characteristics as a teacher, using the lists provided in this chapter.

Compare your own rating with the one you gave Jesus.

20

SUMMARY

What are the advantages of a summary?

What are the difficulties in reading a summary without having first read the pages summarized?

What is a summary?

How would you summarize the essential points in the preceding chapters?

The teaching situation is complex, though it may easily be resolved into its essential elements: teacher, student, lesson, aim of teacher, method of teaching, and environment.

The conversation of Jesus with the woman of Samaria is an object lesson in teaching in all these respects.

Jesus began by winning attention through openers that centered on students' interests; then he established some point of contact with his hearers on the physical or spiritual plane.

As a teacher he was not only a tactician with methods but also a strategist with objectives. His greatest objective was to share with people that sense of union with the Father that he enjoyed.

Jesus based his teaching on the vital problems in the lives of his students.

Though he was not a Greek, he was as ready to converse in a profitable way as was Socrates, and he led a more public life, though shorter, than did Socrates.

He asked and answered questions to stimulate self-expression, desiring conviction rather than persuasion on the part of his followers. His questions are better than those of Socrates because they are mostly of a kind other than leading.

He used the discourse at many different times before many different groups on many different themes, but always in a more or less informal way.

He told stories with a point, the parables, which his listeners did not always understand but which always made them think and led the spiritually minded to inquire into their meaning.

He knew and used the Old Testament Scriptures, both for the needs of his own soul and as a common meeting ground with the religious minds of his day.

He never let an occasion slip but utilized it as it arose to clarify thought and to guide life.

The principle of true learning is recognized in his words: "He who has ears, let him hear," and all his parables present the less familiar in terms of the more familiar. Even so, he was often misunderstood.

He used the principle of contrast to make real the portrayal of truth, concrete examples to bring the abstract near, symbols to make, if possible, difficult meanings plain, and wonderful imagery to enhance the appeal to the imagination and so to lead people to conviction.

He cared more for individuals than for crowds, though he would often minister to crowds, perhaps with a view to reaching individuals.

He trained his disciples as witnesses of him, by personal association, individualizing instruction, and meeting the needs of each one.

The work accomplished by Jesus and through others, under his tutelage, was based on high motivation because of the awakening of spiritual and altruistic impulses rather than those of personal advancement.

In a most interesting way, Jesus probed the depths of human nature and touched on most of the innate reactions of man, though some, like rivalry, he did not consciously appeal to, and some, like sex, he sublimated.

All the methods of impression he used were but means to expression. Jesus was far more pragmatic than either idealistic or mystic.

Jesus appreciated childhood and made its characteristics identical with those of membership in the kingdom.

In a way not surprising but confirming our previous impressions, Jesus embodies those qualities of the teacher commonly set up as ideal.

As we followed these discussions we doubtless discovered repeatedly that the problems of teaching that we ourselves face are similar to those that Jesus faced and that the solutions he found will greatly assist us in our work.

Jesus is the master teacher. Have we made him ours?

21

JESUS IN EDUCATIONAL HISTORY

At the end of a study like this, dealing with Jesus as the great teacher, you would like to know how the historians of education have presented Jesus, those people whose business it is to record systematically past educational events of worthwhile significance and so to make possible the understanding of the present educational situation in the light of the past.

Sadly, among the thousands and thousands of people who have written about Jesus' teaching for more than two thousand years, it is almost impossible to find a single writer who understood the difference between the content of Jesus' teaching and the ways in which he taught. Only within the last hundred years do we find people beginning to distinguish between these two fundamental aspects of Jesus' work.

One may properly wonder why this is so. Why do historians of education, like the inn at Bethlehem, have no room for him? One can only guess at the answer. It is not through the failure to recognize the importance of Christianity in the world but the failure to sense the significance of Jesus as a teacher among the teachers of the world. This failure may be due to the obscuring of the historical figure of Jesus as teacher by an awareness of his divinity, and hence a real difficulty of discovering and presenting the great teacher of Nazareth. Furthermore, those who are interested in education have not always known about Jesus, and those interested in Jesus have not known about education.

P. V. N. Painter in his *History of Education*, published in 1897, was one of the first to recognize Jesus as a teacher, one who was a model for teachers today, not just a perfect person beyond our reach.[1] Painter points out that we can look at Jesus as a teacher in the same way we look at other great teachers. He then goes on to identify some of the features that distinguish Jesus' pedagogy — sympathy, adaptation to the capacity of his hearers, use of outward circumstances, expectation of a gradual development, and insisting only on practical and fundamental truths.

By the time of World War I several books had appeared dealing with Jesus' approach to teaching. Patrick J. McCormick, a Roman Catholic educator, was one of the more articulate of these writers.[2] In his *History of Education* McCormick described Jesus as presenting a twofold approach to the needs and conditions of the time. First, the general adaptation of sublime and abstract truths to the capacity of the human intelligence; second, the particular application of these truths to individual instances. He goes on to point out that Jesus modeled what he taught.

Throughout this early part of the twentieth century, parallel to the growing literature on Jesus as a teacher, Herman Harrell Horne was actively writing and speaking on the same subject, culminating in his classic work of 1920, *Jesus, the Master Teacher*.[3] Horne's work marked the end of the recovery phase that began toward the end of the nineteenth century. After 1920 there was no longer any confusion over the place of Jesus as a teacher, one who could be a model for any and every classroom teacher.

Unfortunately, throughout the 1920s and continuing into the 1950s, the dominant influence of John Dewey's philosophy of education hindered the adoption of Jesus' pedagogy. Even after the publication of Horne's *The Democratic Philosophy of Education*, in which he fully exposed the weaknesses in Dewey's outlook, it took the launch of the Soviet Union's "Sputnik" in 1957 to open the minds of educational leaders to new approaches to learning.[4]

By 1960, whole chapters of educational texts were being devoted to Jesus' ways of teaching. One example is Frederick Mayer's *A History of Educational Thought*.[5] Like Horne, Mayer compares Jesus with other great educators and thus places him in the mainstream of educational history. He singles out individual care as one of the hallmarks of Jesus' teaching. He then goes on to say that, as is evident in Jesus' life, real education is existential, demanding a living encounter between teacher and student.

Endnotes

1. P. V. N. Painter, *A History of Education* (New York: D. Appleton and Company), 1897.

2. Patrick J. McCormick, *History of Education* (Washington, D.C.: The Catholic Education Press, 1915).
3. H. H. Horne, *Jesus, the Master Teacher* (New York: Association Press, 1920).
4. H. H. Horne, *The Democratic Philosophy of Education* (New York: Macmillan, 1932).
5. Frederick Mayer, *A History of Educational Thought* (Columbus, Ohio: Merrill Books, 1960).

BIBLIOGRAPHY

Austin, Gilbert R., and Herbert Garber, eds. *Research on Exemplary Schools.* London: Academic Press, 1985.

Barclay, W. *Educational Ideals in the Ancient World.* London: Collins, 1959.

Burron, Arnold, and John Eidsmoe. *Christ in the Classroom: The Christian Teacher and the Public School.* Denver: Accent, 1987.

Curtis, S. J., and M. E. A. Boultwood, eds. *A Short History of Educational Ideas.* London: University Tutorial Press Ltd., 1953.

Curtis, W. A. *Jesus Christ the Teacher: The Study of His Method and Message Based Mainly on the Earlier Gospels.* London: Oxford University Press, 1943.

Derrett, J. M. *Jesus' Audience: The Social and Psychological Environment in Which He Worked.* London: Darton, Longman, and Todd, 1973.

Dixon, R. G. Des. *Future Schools and How to Get There from Here.* Toronto: E C W, 1992.

Friedeman, M. *The Master Plan of Teaching.* Wheaton: Victor, 1990.

Hill, Brian V. *The Greening of Christian Education.* Homebush West, Australia: Lancer, 1985.

Horne, H. H. (major publications only)

_____. *The Philosophy of Education.* New York: Macmillan, 1904.

_____. *Psychological Principles of Education.* New York: Macmillan, 1906.

_____. *Idealism in Education.* New York: Macmillan, 1910.

_____. *Free Will and Human Responsibility.* New York: Macmillan, 1912.

_____. *Story Telling, Questioning, and Studying.* New York: Macmillan, 1916.

_____. *Jesus Our Standard.* New York: Abingdon, 1918.

_____. *Modern Problems as Jesus Saw Them.* New York: Association Press, 1918.

_____. *Jesus, the Master Teacher.* New York: Association Press, 1920.

_____. *Christ in Man-making.* New York: Abingdon, 1925.

_____. *This New Education.* New York: Abingdon, 1931.

_____. *The Essentials of Leadership.* Nashville: Cokesbury, 1931.

_____. *The Democratic Philosophy of Education.* New York: Macmillan, 1932.

_____. *The Philosophy of Christian Education.* New York: Revell, 1937.

Kealy. John P. *Jesus the Teacher.* Denville, N.J.: Dimension, 1978.

Leslie, R. C. *Jesus and Logotherapy: The Ministry of Jesus as Interpreted Through the Psychotherapy of Victor Frankl.* New York: Abingdon, 1965.

Loretan, J. O., and S. Umans. *Teaching the Disadvantaged.* New York: Columbia University Press, 1966.

McCormick, Patrick J. *History of Education.* Washington, D.C.: The Catholic Education Press, 1915.

Manson, T. W. *The Teaching of Jesus: Studies of Its Form and Content.* Cambridge: Cambridge University Press, 1951.

Marrou, H. I. *A History of Education in Antiquity.* London: Sheed and Ward, 1956.

Mayer, Frederick. *A History of Educational Thought.* Columbus, Ohio: Merrill Books, 1960.

Painter, P. V. N. *A History of Education.* New York: D. Appleton and Company, 1897.

Perkins, P. *Jesus as Teacher.* Cambridge: Cambridge University Press, 1990.

Reader's Digest Association. *Jesus and His Times.* Pleasantville, N.Y.: Reader's Digest, 1987.

Sharman, H. B. *Jesus as Teacher.* New York: Harper and Brothers, 1935.

Sidey, K., ed. *The Blackboard Fumble.* Wheaton: Victor, 1989.

Silver, F. M. *City as a Classroom.* New York: Teaching Resources, 1977.

Stein, R. H. *The Method and Message of Jesus' Teaching.* Philadelphia: Westminster, 1978.

Stevens, George Barker. *The Teaching of Jesus.* New York: Macmillan, 1902.

Weigle, L. A. *Jesus and the Educational Method.* New York: Abingdon, 1939.

Wilson, C. A. *Jesus the Teacher.* Melbourne: Hill of Content Publications, 1974.